In naming this book
ROGER KAPUTNIK AND GOD,
many people asked,
"WHO'S HE?"
Funny how few people
know who
GOD
is.

More Humor from SIGNET

ROGER KAPUTNIK AND GOD

Written
and
Illustrated
by
Dave Berg

EDITED BY
Jerry De Fuccio

A SIGNET BOOK
NEW AMERICAN LIBRARY
TIMES MIRROR

Copyright © 1974 by Dave Berg

 SIGNET TRADEMARK REG. U.S. PAT. OFF. AND FOREIGN COUNTRIES
REGISTERED TRADEMARK—MARCA REGISTRADA
HECHO EN CHICAGO, U.S.A.

SIGNET, SIGNET CLASSICS, MENTOR,
PLUME and MERIDIAN BOOKS
are published by The New American Library, Inc.
1301 Avenue of the Americas, New York, New York 10019

First Printing, October, 1974

1 2 3 4 5 6 7 8 9

PRINTED IN THE UNITED STATES OF AMERICA

So much ungodliness has been done
in the name of GOD that one
more piece of ungodliness won't
break the straw on the camel's back.

Therefore I dedicate this book to
        GOD.
I thank HIM for letting us live
in a land where our supermarket
shopping carts, like King David's cup,
        RUNNETH OVER.

**WITH GRATEFUL
ACKNOWLEDGMENT TO:**

WILLIAM M. GAINES, publisher of *MAD*
magazine, for allowing the reprinting of some of
the author's *MAD* illustrations. Mr. Gaines
believes that GOD does not exist, yet he
arranged for these two books about GOD to be
written, then disclaimed them. Gaines physically
looks like a blending of Michelangelo's rendition
of GOD and Moses. Mr. Gaines also disclaims
Michelangelo.

**WITH GRATEFUL
ACKNOWLEDGMENT TO:**

JERRY DE FUCCIO, who edited this book,
though he is not on the Signet Staff.
Mr. De Fuccio is an associate editor of an
unnamed *ferschluginer* magazine published by a
man who looks like a blending of Michelangelo's
rendition of GOD and Moses. Jerry believes
there is a GOD, but he does not believe
William M. Gaines exists. However, he does
believe in Mr. Gaines' disclaimer.

**WITH GRATEFUL
ACKNOWLEDGMENT TO:**

THE REVEREND DR. VERNARD ELLER,
who wrote the foreword to this book.
Reverend Eller believes there is a GOD, a
William M. Gaines, a Jerry De Fuccio—but
believes that the author does not exist.

WITH GRATEFUL ACKNOWLEDGMENT TO:

RABBI JACOB SHANKMAN, at whose Bible Breakfast discussions the author took notes, while the others attending ate bagels and lox. Had the others taken notes instead of eating, the good Rabbi would be disclaiming their books instead of Berg's. Rabbi Shankman believes in GOD, William M. Gaines, Jerry De Fuccio, Reverend Dr. Vernard Eller—but he believes that this book does not exist.

*   *   *   *

FOREWORD
And, Hopefully, Upward

I never did express any doubt that Dave Berg *exists*. All I said, upon first meeting him, was, "What hath God wrought?"

A Voice broke in, "*Who* wrought?"

Dave insists that the words were, "Hoo Rah!"—but I know what I heard. I also heard tell that a Rabbinical College made Dave an Honorary Rabbi.

Dave Berg is about as much of a Jewish Rabbi as I am—and that's saying something. I'm a Christian preacher-type; and he's . . . well, he's a MADman. (By the way, do you know how the American Heritage Dictionary defines "MAD"? "Airport code for Madrid, Spain." That's a bigger laugh than anything I've seen in MAD.)

Now "Rabbi" is the Jewish term meaning "teacher"; and I *am* a teacher of religion (*Christian* religion) at La Verne College. Dave tried his hand at teaching religion (*Jewish* religion) with MY FRIEND GOD, the predecessor of this book. He admits that it excited many more compliments from Christians than from Jews. That shows how good a Rabbi he is; he makes his best pitch and winds up selling the "Brand X" religion.

Granted, in many ways Dave would seem to be more *Jewish* that I am. Yet, every chance he gets, he makes a point of telling me that all Christians are actually Jews. He thinks that will make me mad. It doesn't. I knew that long before he thought he invented the idea; Christian scripture says as much. (However, he wouldn't be so quick to keep saying this if he once considered the implication: If I'm a *Jew,* I've got all the religion he's got . . . PLUS.)

As two Jewish Rabbis, then, we're in business together—the Minister and the MADman. The only real difference is that Berg uses much more of capital letters and boldface type than I do. I don't have to **SHOUT** when I preach.

What it all comes to, then, is that—whether you be Semite, pro-Semite, anti-Semite, semi-Semite, or not-a-mite-Semite—this book is YOURS (*after* you pay for it, Dum-Dum!).

My reward for writing the foreword, Dave tells me, is that I get to list the titles of all *my* books. "What? And have all you dear readers put this kaputnik book back on the rack and rush off looking for mine?" Better he should have *paid* me! But if that is all he knows, here goes: The MAD Morality / The Sex Manual for Puritans / King Jesus' Manual of Arms for the 'Armless / The Simple Life / The Most Revealing Book of the Bible / and others too numerous (and too good) to mention here.

VERNARD KAPUTNIK ELLER
La Verne College, California

ROGER KAPUTNIK AND GOD

IN THE BEGINNING
GOD CREATED THE WHOLE MEGILLAH

The question is,
"WHO IS ROGER KAPUTNIK?"
It's a name I use in *MAD* magazine and in the *MAD* books.
My mother raised four children and a cat.
Harold, Milton, Naomi, Schnitzel, and Whatshisname.
When she wanted to call me, she'd yell,
"HAROLD, I mean **MILTON,** I mean **NAOMI,** I mean **SCHNITZEL** (who was the cat), I mean **WHATSHISNAME."**
I'M "WHATSHISNAME."
One day when she was running down the list, I suggested,
"Try ROGER KAPUTNIK."
THAT name she could remember.
If you think my mother was a bad name-caller, you ought to hear my sister.
When she wants to call me, she yells,
"HAROLD, I mean **MILTON,** I mean **NAOMI** (which is **HER** name),
I mean **SCHNITZEL** (who departed thirty years ago),
I mean **GEORGE,** I mean **BOBBY,** I mean **MARK,** I mean **KENNY,**
I mean **MITCH,** I mean **NANCY,** I mean **WHATSHIS-NAME."**
And I say, "Try **ROGER KAPUTNIK!"**
THAT name she remembers.
Nobody in my family can remember my name.
Neither can I.
I had to look it up.
According to my birth certificate,
it's **DAVID.**
According to the Bible,
it means **BELOVED.**
According to my family,
it's **FORGETTABLE.**

* * * *

So who is **ROGER KAPUTNIK?**
I'm not the only one.
It's every **KLUTZ, BOOB, SCHLEMIEL,**
and **SAP** in the world.
So who is **ROGER KAPUTNIK?**
Every person who **UNDERWHELMS** anyone.

Anybody about whom people say:
"I can never remember a name,
but your **FACE,** that I can't remember either."
Roger Kaputnik is the most
FORGETTABLE character anyone ever met.
When he goes through an electric eye,
the door **DOESN'T OPEN.**
He leads a **FULL EMPTY LIFE.**
But Roger Kaputnik looks
great on **RADIO.**
Roger Kaputniks are
CLOSET HETEROSEXUALS.
Roger Kaputnik is never our real name.
Our real name is
"LEGION."

*   *   *   *

While lecturing to a college audience
I made the statement,
"The reason that the television
show **'ALL IN THE FAMILY'** is so
popular is because we are
all **IDENTIFYING** with the bigot
Archie Bunker. **BEHIND THAT
PHONY LIBERALISM WE ARE
ALL A BUNCH OF RACIST BIGOTED
PIGS!"**
One student
angrily disagreed with me.
he shouted,

13

**"WE ARE NOT A BUNCH OF
BIGOTED RACIST PIGS,
YOU GOD DAMN JEW BASTARD
SHEENY KIKE!"
THIS COULD ONLY HAPPEN TO A ROGER
KAPUTNIK.**

*   *   *   *

If a Roger is **UNKLUTZY** enough
to win a **GOLD MEDAL**,
he's so proud of it
that he has it **BRONZED**.

Roger says,

"He who steals my purse,
steals **CASH**."

A Roger Kaputnik is a
living unknown soldier.
He is a clerical error.
When he receives mail, it's always
addressed to **OCCUPANT**
with postage due yet.

Roger gets blackballed
at every club he tries to join,
so he joins a club made up
of only those who get blackballed,
AND STILL GETS BLACKBALLED.

The statistics show
the average family has
two and a half children,
ROGER IS THE HALF.

When Roger Kaputnik is young
HE KNOWS EVERYTHING ABOUT EVERYTHING.
As he gets older
He knows that **HE DOESN'T KNOW.**
TO KNOW THAT YOU DON'T KNOW
IS TO KNOW.
In time he gets to know
MORE and **MORE**
about **LESS** and **LESS**
until he knows
EVERYTHING ABOUT NOTHING.

*   *   *   *

A Roger Kaputnik is very often a
NICE GUY.
Really more of a
SCHNOOK
than **NICE,** but still **NICE.**
WHO NEEDS NICE GUYS?
With a **ROTTEN GUY**
you know exactly what to expect,
HE'S ROTTEN.
When a **ROTTEN GUY** is **ROTTEN**
to a **NICE GUY**
what does the **NICE GUY** do?
HE'S NICE
to the **ROTTEN GUY.**
Which **HURTS** the **ROTTEN GUY.**
Which makes the **ROTTEN GUY** feel **ASHAMED.**
Which makes the **ROTTEN GUY** feel **ROTTEN.**
Which is a **ROTTEN THING** for a **NICE GUY**
to do.
SO BEING NICE
IS BEING MORE ROTTEN
THAN BEING ROTTEN.

*   *   *   *

OPEN LETTER TO ALL THE JEWS OF THE WORLD.
I keep hearing from non-Jews that
**THERE IS A SECRET JEWISH PLOT TO TAKE OVER
THE WORLD.**
What I want to know is:
So, how come I'm **NOT GETTING A
PIECE OF THE ACTION?**
HOW COME NOBODY TOLD ME ABOUT IT?
**HOW COME NOBODY GAVE ME MY INSTRUCTIONS
ON HOW TO GO ABOUT TAKING THE TAKING OVER?**
AM I SUCH A NON-PERSON?
AM I SUCH A NEBBISH?
AM I SUCH A ROGER KAPUTNIK?

Yes I am.
I don't even want to be president
of the club I belong to,
AND I'M THE ONLY MEMBER.
But still, if there's such a secret plot, the least
you can do is let me in on it
SO I CAN KEEP OUT OF THE WAY.
Maybe this secret Jewish plot
is so secret that no Jew
knows the secret.
Only those who aren't Jewish seem
to know it.
So I write an
OPEN LETTER TO ALL NON-JEWS OF THE WORLD
Who say, **THERE'S A JEWISH PLOT TO TAKE
OVER THE WORLD.**
What I want to know is
**SO HOW COME WE JEWS ARE NOT GETTING
A PIECE OF THE ACTION?**

*   *   *   *

A Roger hears that
**"THERE'S AN EXCEPTION
TO EVERY RULE."**
Therefore he calculates
by this rule,
there must be **ONE** rule
that **DOESN'T** have an exception.

Roger has a tendency to make
social visits at the most
inopportune times—
WHEN YOU ARE HOME.

He is the type who swears,
"As **GOD** is my judge—
I'm an **ATHEIST.**"
Of this type of **ATHEIST,** Oscar Levant
said, "He has no **INVISIBLE MEANS OF SUPPORT.**"

Roger Kaputnik loves **DRIVE-IN** movies,
especially the
MATINEES.
He doesn't have fun while he's having
A GOOD TIME.
When they say,
"People who need love the most
are the least lovable,"
they mean Roger.

A Roger Kaputnik is not a
very good money manager.
The only way a Roger
can make it on a **MIDDLE-CLASS
INCOME**
is to be a
MILLIONAIRE.

A Roger reads a poem from
an unknown author in the Warsaw Ghetto Newspaper,
translated in the hell year of 1942 by Marie Syrkin.

From tomorrow on, I shall be sad
From tomorrow on!
Today I shall be gay.
What is the use of sadness—tell me that?—
Because these evil winds begin to blow?

Why should I grieve for tomorrow—today?
Tomorrow may be so good, so sunny,
Tomorrow the sun may shine for us again,
We will no longer need to be sad.
From tomorrow on, I shall be sad,
From tomorrow on!
Not today; no, today I will be glad,
And every day, no matter how bitter it be,
I shall say;
From tomorrow on, I shall be sad,
Not today!

Roger Kaputnik reads this
lovely poem
and thinks about the poet who
wrote this beautiful sad verse—
"From tomorrow on, I shall be sad."
And Roger is
SAD TODAY.
He can't wait until tomorrow.

*   *   *   *

The poets speak of the joy of children's laughter
at play.
D'j'ever hear the laughter of children at play
in a playground?
The laughs come in the form of **SHRIEKS, SCREAMS,
CRIES OF INDIGNATION AND PAIN, LIKE:**
"HE HIT ME FIRST, after I hit him,"
and **"IT'S MINE!"** when it's not.
KIDS are the **CRUELEST PEOPLE IN THE WORLD,**
except for **ADULTS.**
Mothers watching their children at play,
play games themselves, like:
"Your son is hitting my son. Tell him to stop."
"No, I don't interfere in children's arguments."
"Now my son is hitting **YOUR** son."
"NOW I'LL INTERFERE!"

Playgrounds are not for play.
They are for training. They are obstacle courses
for the inner shrieks, screams, cries
of indignation and pain that the
forty-year-old kids have to endure.

England may have won her battles
on the playing fields of Eton,
but in America, it's on the **PLAYGROUNDS**
where the Kaputnik kids
LOST
the battle
and became
HOPELESS NEUROTICS.

*   *   *   *

You're someplace
and you see someone,
but he's in the wrong place.
He's out of context,
and you go through all the mental
gyrations trying to put him in the
right place where you know him
from.
Then the next day you
see him in the right place.
He's the waiter who waits
on you every day at lunch,
or the clerk behind the counter
where you buy your paper,
or the teller at the bank
you talk to once a week.
People who can't be
remembered when they
are out of their natural settings,
always have the same name.
It's Roger Kaputnik.

* * * *

Girls are also Roger Kaputniks
NAMED REGINA.
A Regina has to make omelets
in order to **BREAK EGGS.**
She is the **EVIL**
of **TWO LESSERS.**
There are things that happen
to a Regina **ONCE IN A LIFETIME—**
MANY TIMES.
She'd give her **RIGHT ARM**
to be **AMBIDEXTROUS.**
She is a **SOUL SURVIVOR.**
She sees the **TUNNEL** at the **END OF THE LIGHT.**
Reginas'can be so retiring
that they even have an **UNLISTED ZIP CODE.**

Reginas are the most **UNUSUAL**
people on this planet.
When you look at a Regina
the only thing you see that is
ALIVE
are her **EYES.**
SKIN, HAIR, and **FINGERNAILS**
are **DEAD CELLS.**
Hey, you're that way, too!
Hey!. . . . So am I.
Not only that . . .
Reginas always live in the **PAST.**
A **NOVA** is a star that has exploded
THOUSANDS OF YEARS AGO.
Yet it's only reaching us **NOW.**
When Regina gets angry and
EXPLODES NOW,
we actually don't get to **SEE** and **HEAR**
her until a **SPLIT SECOND LATER.**

Come to think about it—
WE ARE ALL ALWAYS LIVING IN THE PAST.
NONE OF US CAN CATCH UP TO THE PRESENT.
MY GOD! WE ARE ALL THE MOST UNUSUAL
PEOPLE ON THIS PLANET.
We are **ALL REGINA KAPUTNIKS.**

* * * *

A Roger is a
"GIRL WATCHER"
and dreams dreams
that make the red devil blush.
A Regina Kaputnik
dresses provocatively
with a see-through blouse,
short tight skirt,
walks with a jiggle
that makes the red Roger blush.
Then she calls Roger a
"A LECHEROUS MALE CHAUVINIST."

* * * *

Ten—nine—eight—seven—six—five—four—three—two—one . . .

. . . blast off!

BING BONG

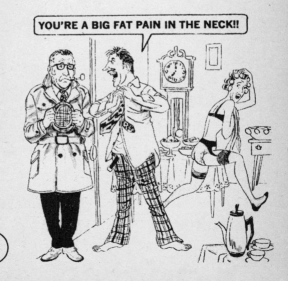

Willy Shakespeare said:
"A rose by any other name would smell
as sweet."
What does Willy know?
Just because he was the greatest writer
since the authors of the Bible?
If a **ROSE** were called a **CRUDSTUNK**,
the effect would not be the same.
If you held that velvety, delicate, colorful,
aromatic flower to your nose,
and someone called it a **CRUDSTUNK**,
the word would clunk on the eardrum,
and psyche out your nose membrane.
It wouldn't smell like a rose at all,
it would smell like a
CRUDSTUNK.

So names **ARE** important.
The very name **ROGER KAPUTNIK**
denotes a **SCHNOOK**.
And only a **SCHNOOK** could pick
such a **SCHNOOKY** name.
First names in the Western world
are called **CHRISTIAN** names.

Names like John, James,
Deborah, and Mary,
which are **HEBREW** names.
Adolf Hitler's father was illegitimate.
He bore his mother's name,
Schicklgruber.
Late in his life, Adolf's illegitimate
grandfather legally adopted his illegitimate
son and gave him the name
Hitler.
**IN THAT VERY ACT, HISTORY WAS DRASTICALLY
        CHANGED.**

Thirty million people would not have been
killed during the Thirties and Forties.
What German could say,
"HAIL, SCHICKLGRUBER!"
without breaking up and laughing?

The riddle is:
"What man born in Georgia became leader
of a large East European country?"
The answer is:
JOSEF VISSARIONOVICH DZHUGASHVILI.
And you say, **"WHO?"**
With that Kaputnik-type name,
he never would have made it.
So he changed it to **STEEL,**
or **STALIN.**
THAT'S who.
The job of Premier of the **USSR** didn't pay enough.
So Stalin had to moonlight as a
BUTCHER.
It is estimated he **BUTCHERED** as many as
FIFTY MILLION PEOPLE.
PEOPLE in **PEOPLE'S DEMOCRACIES**
don't seem to **LIKE PEOPLE.**
Nor are **PEOPLE'S DEMOCRACIES—**
DEMOCRACIES.

At one time, one third of the human race
worshipped a man named
SIDDHARTHA GUATAMA.
So you say, **"YOU GOTTA BE KIDDIN'."**
YES, I AM.
They didn't worship him by **THAT** name.
NO ONE could **PRONOUNCE** it, including the
people from his hometown of **KAPILAVASTU.**
But they **COULD** say
GUATAMA

27

or
ENLIGHTENED
or
BUDDHA.

We are told
there once was a **RABBI JOSHUA BEN JOSEPH**.
He lived and died an **OBSERVING** Jew.
While the good Rabbi Joshua Ben Joseph
seldom said anything that his fellow Jews
hadn't already heard—
HE DID SAY IT BETTER.
He wore a full beard because it is written
in Leviticus that Jews were not to
shape the corner of their beards.
His general image is that of a man
of love and peace.
Yet he was prone at times to militancy and
violence.
Occasionally he was impatient with his friends
and the gentiles.
Yet in time Rabbi Joshua Ben Joseph
became an extremely important man
in the gentile world.
This might never have happened if the Greek
Ragoris Kaputnikosis had not changed the Rabbi's
name to **DIVINELY ANOINTED**
or
JESU CHRISTOS

or
JESUS CHRIST,
Of whom Larry Siegel in *MAD* magazine once wrote,
"He was a nice Jewish boy who went into
his father's business."

*   *   *   *

A Roger Kaputnik has a mind
that has a mind of its own.
He always is last on line,
and the first to be called on
when he doesn't know the answer.
When he knows the answers
he never knows the question.
He buys golf shoes
and the spikes are turned
INWARD
He finds a cloud
in every silver lining.
When Abraham Lincoln said,
"But you can't fool all of the people
all of the time,"
he didn't mean Roger Kaputnik.
There is a **WOMEN'S LIBERATION MOVEMENT.**
There is a **GAY LIBERATION MOVEMENT.**
I propose a **ROGER KAPUTNIK LIBERATION
          MOVEMENT.**
**LIBERATION FOR ALL THE SCHLEMIELS, JERKS,
HAS-BEENS** and **NEVER-WASES,** and **THOSE-WHO-
          WILL-NEVER-BE**
MOVEMENT.
OUR CRY IS
"RIGHT ON—BACKWARD!"

*   *   *   *

FAMOUS UNKNOWNS

WHATHISNAME IS FAMOUS FOR WHAT HE DIDN'T DO

EACH STORY TOLD IN THIS CHAPTER HAS A BASIS OF FACT IN HISTORY. THE AUTHOR HAS TAKEN A CERTAIN **LIBERTY** AND **JUSTICE** TO **ALMOST** ALL.

BERG

When General Bonaparte was marching through
            Egypt
and he came upon the sight of the Pyramids and
Sphinx, the egomaniac General wished to prove
what great cannoneers he had. Bonaparte ordered a
demonstration. The artillerymen took careful aim—
and fired! Blew the nose right off the Sphinx's face.
The marksman in charge of the shoot was
SERGEANT PIERRE KAPUTNIK.
HE WAS AIMING AT THE PYRAMIDS.
Those whom the **GODS** would destroy
they first drive **MAD.**
Those who destroy are **MAD.**
In their madness they
have delusions of grandeur.
Usually they think of themselves
as **JESUS CHRIST** or **NAPOLEON.**
The madman who defaced
Michelangelo's masterpiece **"PIETA"**
said he was **"JESUS CHRIST."**
When **GENERAL BONAPARTE**
defaced
or **DENOSED**
the **SPHINX,**
he said he was
NAPOLEON!

*   *   *   *

The sculptor Michelangelo had a biblical name
meaning Michael the Archangel.
But he didn't know his Bible.
In his famous statue of the young Jew David,
he chiseled him
UNCIRCUMCISED.
Before he studied sculpturing,
he should first have studied how to be a
MOEL (a professional circumciser).
A great talent he was, but an archangel he was not.
He was just a Rogerangelo.
That wasn't the only goof he made.
In the statue of another Jew named
Moses, he put horns on his head.
With David he didn't remove anatomical portions.
With Moses he added on.
Was this the Italian sculptor's goof?
No, it was the goof of another Italian
named **JEROME,** which translates to
GERONIMO in **APACHE.**
He would have made a better Indian
than an Italian scholar.
In the year 386, Jerome settled in Bethlehem
to learn Hebrew, so he could translate
the Old Testament into Latin.
He translated like an Apache.
Jerome did a hatchet job on the Bible.
Ferinstance, it says in the Bible that when
Moses came down from Mount Sinai
with two heavy stone tablets
his face **"SHONE."**
It might be interpreted as meaning he turned
red and glistened with sweat from the heavy burden
he carried.
The biblical word is **"KORAN"**
from the root word **"KEREN,"**

meaning **"TO SHINE"** or **"A RAY OF LIGHT."**
This word can be mistaken for
a similar word meaning **"HORN."**
Jerome, of course, was mistaken,
which explains why Michelangelo
puts horns on the statue of Moses.
For translating the **BIBLE** poorly
he was canonized **ST. JEROME.**
It should have been
ST. ROGER.
For translating Hebrew poorly,
my old Hebrew teacher would
have made Jerome translate it
again and again
until he got it right.
Then my old Hebrew teacher
would not have sainted him—
he would have **BAR-MITZVAHED HIM.**

*   *   *   *

There once reigned a King Louie
With a number after his name.
In those days they only computerized
sovereigns.
His Majesty was slovenly about the
peasants' dress,
but meticulous about his palace guards.
On that history-changing day,
Louie with a number after his name
looked at Private Rogé with a
Kaputnik after his name.
The soldier stood stiffly at attention.
His brass breast buttons glistened.
The black buttons on his white leggings
were neatly in a vertical row.
This was the age before the invention of
JAMMED ZIPPERS.

Louie looked and qvelled.
Just then Private Rogé's nose
began to leak.
In one quick movement the soldier
used the cuff of his uniform to
wipe the dripping beak.
Louie went into a royal tantrum
and ordered that
**HENCEFORTH ALL CUFFS WILL
HAVE LARGE KNOBBY BUTTONS
SO THAT NO MORE NOSE-WIPING
COULD OCCUR.**
And **HENCEFORTH IT WAS.**
To this very day most
men's coats have useless
ridiculous buttons on their cuffs.
All because Private Rogé had
a leaky **SCHNOZZLE.**
One wonders much and ponders more.
**WHAT WOULD MEN'S STYLES BE LIKE
IF PRIVATE ROGE HAD
AN ITCHY TUSSHY.**

*   *   *   *

30 days has September, April, June
and November.
40 **DAYS** has the Bible,
Genesis, Exodus and Ad Infinible.
40 **DAYS** did **NOAH,** with kin and pets,
take a long weekend cruise.
40 **YEARS** did **MOSES** take
on an overnight hike through the desert.
40 **DAYS** did Moses spend on Mount Sinai
to receive only 10 **COMMANDMENTS.**
At that rate the average was ¼ of a
        COMMANDMENT daily.
40 **DAYS** in the wilderness did Jesus
have a **DEVIL** of a time.
40 **DAYS** between **GOOD FRIDAY**
and when some people give up
RELIGION for Lent.
And so it goes on,
40 **DAYS** in the **BOOK OF JONAH,**
40 **DAYS** of **FULFILLMENT,**
and 40 **DAYS** it took me
to find all the 40 **DAYS.**
But why **THAT** particular number?
The answer is—
HOW THE HELL SHOULD I KNOW?
There is, however, a very old legend
I just made up.
Several thousand years ago, there appeared
an item in the ancient Hebrew *Times* stating:
"**WANTED:** Young man, age 25, to be a scribe
on the **BIBLE.**
Must have 40 **YEARS** experience."
One applicant named Roger Bar Copeputnik,
was 40 years of age, and had only 25 years
        experience.
These sets of digits were the closest any job-
        seeker came to the requirements.

So Roger got the job.
He had a failing. Bar Copeputnik could not
cope with numbers.
He was a copeless case.
It took Roger a very long time to reach
40 years of age.
Longer than it took most people.
So he had a 40-year hang-up.
While gathering information about the Spoken Bible,
Rog found that the old story-tellers spoke
of such and such an event taking a long time.
To Rog a long time was 40.
So Roger the Scribe began the
practice of using the number 40 to designate
"A LONG TIME"
which was to continue on into the New Testament.
Thus ends the very old legend I'm sorry
I just made up from historical fragments.
Yet is not there some truth that 40
is a comparatively long time?
To a woman, the age between 39
and 40 takes at least 10 years.
To this day there are some theologians
who accept the above theory
after trying 40 other theories.

Let us be grateful that Roger and the Scribe
did not write the calendar.
Otherwise it would read:
"40 **DAYS** has September, April, June, and
        November,
**ALL THE REST
ARE MESSED.**"

*   *   *   *

A member of the National Riflemen's
Association, named Roger Gunther Kaputnik,
was a loud advocate of the right
to bear arms.
Anti-gunners just as loudly denounced
guns for being used to kill important personages,
unimportant shopkeepers, and even
less important beautiful animals.
AND GUNS SHOULD BE OUTLAWED.
Roger Gunther Kaputnik shot back with,
"GUNS DON'T KILL PEOPLE,
PEOPLE KILL PEOPLE.
SO DON'T OUTLAW GUNS,
OUTLAW PEOPLE."

       *   *   *   *

The **PRIMROSE PATH**
refers to the path leading to
the **DEVIL.**
It was named after the
man who spoke the most
AGAINST these kind of activities.
His name was the Reverend Primrose.
To be remembered for the
exact **OPPOSITE** of what he stood for
shows that he had a lot of
Roger Kaputnik in him.
It should have been called
the **KAPUTNIK PATH.**

       *   *   *   *

There is talk going around that when
the **DEAD SEA SCROLLS WERE FOUND,**
they also unearthed a very old **TAPE RECORDING.**
So you say, "That's **RIDICULOUS.** They didn't
have **TAPE RECORDINGS** in those days."
Why not? After all, what is a tape recording
but a **LONG SKINNY SCROLL?**
So you say, "Okay, but they didn't
have **ELECTRICITY."**
We always had electricity.
So you say, "Yeah, but they didn't
KNOW WHAT IT WAS THEN."
Neither do we **NOW.**
So whether it is authentic or not,
these dubious tapes are supposed to be the
happenings of what took place on
that historical day in the year 90
at Jamnia, Palestine.

There, according to the tapes, the
leading Rabbis met to edit the Bible.
Don't tell me they didn't have
editors in those days.
From the time people learned to write,
they've had editors and critics and kibbitzers.
On these tapes they say that
the first voice to be heard was that of
Rabbi Reuven Bar Kaput.
He complained that the Bible was too long.
He could never remember who wrote
the Proverbs and who wrote the Psalms.
Another Rabbi suggested he learn this poem:

"KING DAVID AND KING SOLOMON LED
DIFFERENT KINDS OF LIVES.
THEY CUT UP DIFFERENT DIDOES
WITH DIFFERENT KINDS OF WIVES.
BUT WHEN DEATH APPROACHED THEM,
THEN WITH DIFFERENT QUALMS,
KING SOLOMON WROTE THE PROVERBS,
AND DAVID WROTE THE PSALMS."
Another Rabbi pointed out that it was
impossible for Bar Kaput to learn it—
since **THAT POEM HAD NOT BEEN INVENTED YET.**
Then Rabbi Reuven wished to discuss
**HOW MANY ANGELS COULD DANCE ON THE HEAD
OF A PIN.**
He was overruled.
Instead, they threw out the **BOOK OF MACCABEES.**
Fortunately, the Catholics later picked it
up and made it apocryphal in the Vulgate edition.
Because of that, Jewish children have had
Channukah with eight days of presents to
complain about,
while Christian children only have
one day of Christmas gifts to
complain about.
Again the voice of Rabbi Reuven Bar Kaput
          proposed
they discuss how many
ANGELS CAN DANCE ON THE HEAD OF A PIN.
He was overruled.
Instead the Rabbis threw out some other chapters.
They ended up in that unknown place where
all lost things become loster.
Again the voice of Rabbi Reuven Bar Kaput made
the same proposal.
Again it was overruled.
Then they almost threw out the
Book of **ESTHER** because **GOD** was not mentioned.

Instead, they made it a Megillah, meaning
a **SCROLL.** Today, in American **SLANGUAGE,**
MEGILLAH means the **"WHOLE SMEER."**
Once again Rabbi Reuven Bar Kaput made his
        proposal.
Once again it was overruled.
Instead they almost threw out the
most beautiful love poem ever written,
THE SONG OF SONGS. This because it
suggested **CARNAL LOVE.**
But the Rabbis finally rationalized
that it was all symbolic.
Ferinstance, when the poem speaks
of female breasts, they rationalized
it meant **MOSES** and **AARON**—
without the **BEARDS.**
This time Rabbi Reuven Bar Kaput insisted
that they discuss **HOW MANY ANGELS
CAN DANCE ON THE HEAD OF A PIN.**
They finally shut up the **NUDNICK**
by pointing out that
"THE PIN HAD NOT BEEN INVENTED YET."
So it shouldn't be a total loss,
Rabbi Reuven Bar Kaput proposed that
**"THE BIBLE SHOULD BE CONCLUDED
AND NOTHING MORE BE ADDED."**
This they gave in to,
and the **CONCLUSION** of the Bible
was **CONCLUDED.**
So you see, according to dubious Dead Sea Tapes,
the concluding of the Bible was a decision made
by **MEN, NOT BY GOD.**
So being a Kaputnik-type person,
I make a Kaputnik-type proposal:
**THAT THE BIBLE BE CONTINUED FROM
WHENCE IT LEFT OFF.**

Too many historical facts should be recorded.
Too many **BEGATS** have been **BEGOTTEN.**
I propose we call it the
"NEW OLD TESTAMENT."
We are going through a **GOLDEN AGE
OF JEWISH WRITERS.**
Chaim Potok, Herbert Tarr, Bernard Malamud,
Norman Mailer, Cynthia Ozick, Ed Doctorow,
Ed Cetera, and all the other et ceteras.
I propose that each one of these writers
take a chapter and
VERSE IT.
Chapters such as,
**DIASPORA, CRUSADES, INQUISITION, GHETTO,
SHTETL, POGROMS, THE SIX MILLION, ISRAEL,**
and **VATICAN TWO.**
Of course, this will bring loud objections
from **ORTHODOX RABBIS.**
They will demand that they add more
chapters and verse on just why
**NO MORE CHAPTERS AND VERSES SHOULD BE
          ADDED.**
The Fundamentalist minister will make
the same objection.
Of the Fundamentalists, someone once said.
"They are blind men in a totally dark room,
loooking for a black cat that isn't there,
AND YET THEY FIND THE CAT."
Fundamentalists, do not raise your wrath,
you and I know that the cat had kittens.
The kittens were there.
The objectors to the continuations of the
Bible will once again meet in Jamnia, Israel.
Those future tapes will reveal that
once again, a nudnick Rabbi Roger Kaputwitz
will demand that they first discuss,

**"HOW MANY ANGELS CAN DANCE ON THE HEAD
OF A BALL POINT PEN."**
He will be overruled, then it will be pointed out that,
**"A BALL POINT PEN THAT WORKS WHEN YOU
      REALLY NEED IT,
HASN'T BEEN INVENTED YET."**

*   *   *   *

The story is told about a mighty
movie mogul. Brilliant as a producer
but crude in manner.
At a story conference one
writer named Roger suggested
that they make a movie based
on a Bible story.
**"WHAT THE HELL DO YOU KNOW ABOUT
THE BIBLE?"** the mogul bellowed.
"I know enough," said Roger.
"FIFTY BUCKS," yelled the mogul,
**"SAYS YOU DON'T EVEN KNOW
THE LORD'S PRAYER."**
"You're on," said Roger.
**"NOW I LAY ME DOWN TO SLEEP,
I PRAY THE LORD MY SOUL TO KEEP."**
And the mighty movie mogul said,
"Son of a gun,
I DIDN'T THINK YOU KNEW IT."

*   *   *   *

Long before civilization started—
and may **GOD** grant that it will start soon,
men went into the real estate business.
They didn't buy and sell property with dollars
and cents and make a profit.
They block-busted a territory
and took a loss.
The new tribe, moving in, ran down the
neighborhood.
During one such ancient
urban renewal project, two
tribes fought to a Mexican standoff.
Which was odd, since **MEXICO** had
not yet been invented.
Rogput, the leader of one tribe, wished
to make a deal.
So he stood up in view of the enemy,
while holding his shield in his left hand;
he threw down his spear and held up his
right hand to show he had
NO WEAPON.
And that's how the **PEACE SIGN**
was invented.
The rival real estate dealer
did the same thing.
Both met in no-man's-land.
That's how **CONDEMNED PROPERTY**
was invented.
Still wary, they grabbed each
other's right hand —so that
the fingers could not be used as a weapon.
Then they shook each other's hand
to make sure there were no weapons
up each other's sleeves.
and that's how the **HANDSHAKE**
was invented.

And that's how the **SLEEVE**
was invented.
And that's how an
UNEASY PEACE was invented.
And that's also how **GOD'S**
LITTLE HEART ACRES were invented.
To this day,
still before civilization started,
real estate deals are closed with
a handshake.
This **AFTER** the **WEAPON** has been laid down—
THE PEN,
which they tell us penetrates mightier than
the sword.
So the warmest gesture between
two human-type people, the **HANDSHAKE,**
comes from the result of the most
hostile gesture—**CLOBBERING!**
Which makes of us all **HYPOCRITES.**
Except for **PRIZE FIGHTERS.**
They **CLOBBER** each other
AFTER they've **SHAKEN HANDS.**

*   *   *   *

Many historians believe that Christopher Columbus
was originally a Jew—
But then isn't almost everybody?
They say his real name was **COLON**
or **COLUMBO**.
The ancient Hebrews had a notion
that the world was round.
Columbus **ONLY SECONDED THE NOTION**.
The **JERUSALEM TALMUD** referred
to our world as a **SPHERE**.
Another of the early writings, called the
ZOHAR, actually states that the world
rotated on its axis, and when one half
of the globe was dark, the other half
was light.
The difference between the skeptics and
the Zoharists was like night and day.
The skeptics said Columbus would fall off
the edge of the world.
Actually he did.
He did fall off the edge of the known world
into the Caribbean **TOURIST TRAP**.
Another failing is that Chris
thought he was in the East Indies.
Any schnook would have known he wasn't
in Asia.
None of the natives he met were making
AMERICAN FLAGS marked
"MADE IN JAPAN."
Maybe Chris's real name was **COLPUTNIK**.
The first man of Chris's crew to be
sent ashore was a Jewish sailor
whose name was something like
Roger Torres.
He was sent to confirm Chris's
reservation on the Caribbean resort.

There was an Indian Convention going on
at the time, and they were full up.
However, they suggested he try the Hilton
which should be built any century now.
Torres returned, giving an account
of what he saw.
He described a strange large bird,
which looked something like a peacock.
He called it by its Hebrew name,
"TUKKI."
As a result, when the Hilton was
finally built, American tourists
knew what to order on
THANKSGIVING:
"TUKKI"
or as they say in fractured Hebrew,
"TURKEY."

* * * *

There is a passage in the Old Testament that declares:
"SUFFER YOU NOT A WITCH TO LIVE."
Many Jews interpreted this as meaning,
**"DON'T LET A WITCH MAKE A LIVING OUT OF
        WITCHCRAFT,
LET HER SUFFER BY TAKING YOUR PROBLEM TO
        YOUR AUNT SADIE
INSTEAD, WHO WILL GIVE YOU THE SAME BULL
        FOR NOTHING."**
In the Middle Ages, many Christians interpreted
this passage in an unchristian manner.
Blithely skipping over the commandment,
"THOU SHALT NOT KILL,"
they said, **"THOU SHALT,
BY MAKING HER SUFFER AND NOT LIVE."**
There came a time when the local yentas
accused a Mrs. Regina Walter of being a witch.
This because she made a delicious apple dumpling
for her husband with a
BETTY CROCKER CAKE MIX.
And everybody knew Betty wasn't born yet.
The question arose,
**"HOW DO YOU KNOW FOR SURE THAT A WITCH
IS A WITCH?"**
One Squire Roger Kaputwick said he knew.
"A WITCH CANNOT FLOAT IN WATER."
So the Squire threw Regina into the local pond
and watered Walter.
Weighed down with the heavy burden
of cake mix in her pockets,
she sank to the bottom.
So they dragged her out of the pond
and hung her from the nearest tree,
where she dangled like a participle.
Mr. Walter realizing he was out one good
apple dumpling maker, became enraged.

He grabbed Squire Kaputwick and threw
him into the pond.
Being a real drag, the Squire sank
to the bottom.
The townspeople, being concerned for the
good Squire, pulled him out of the pond.
Then they hung him out to dry . . .
AT THE END OF A ROPE.

* * * *

Two thousand years before **"THE PILL"**
was invented,
the ancient Hebrews invented **"THE PILL"**
called **"THE CUP OF STERILITY."**
It was a concoction of certain secret
herbs mixed in wine. It made both
men and women **TEMPORARILY STERILE.**
But **NOT IMPOTENT.**
In the act of fun games,
they took out the **GAME,**
but not the **FUN.**
GOD DID SAY, "BE FRUITFUL AND MULTIPLY."
So why did the ancient Hebrews forget
their **MULTIPLICATION TABLES?**
Because girls married at the beginning of puberty,
it was not considered safe
for so **YOUNG** a child to have so **YOUNG** a child.
But she was old enough to have the **FUN.**
What determined the age of puberty?
TWO pubic hairs.
Which had to be witnessed by **TWO** people,
ONE for **EACH HAIR.**

This may seem **LEWDISH** to some,
but it comes from the **HOLY TALMUD.**
Those authors were not **LEWDISH,**
they were **PRUDISH.**

So legend says.
The secret formula for the **"CUP OF STERILITY"**
was entrusted to **ONE BOAZ BEN KAPUTNIK**
living in **JERUSALEM** (which means City of Peace.)
One night he put **NOT** enough herbs
and **TOO MUCH** wine in the concoction;
this led to a two-week bender.
When he sobered up, he could very
clearly remember the **WINE**
but not the **HERBS.**
"THE PILL" was lost for two thousand years.
Did that make this Boaz Ben Kaputnik
a **KLUTZ?**
No, for once a Roger Kaputnik was a **HERO.**

Two thousand years later, when another
Roger Kaputnik reinvented **"THE PILL,"**
he **WAS** a **KLUTZ!**
This Roger changed the sexual morals
of the **YET** to be civilized world.
GIRLS could now have "fun" without the
fear of pregnancy.
THEN they get pregnant.
Girls would forget to take "the pill,"
but they didn't forget to
take the **KLUTZ.**
Girls can be Roger Kaputniks also.
The "morning-after pill" was also invented
by another **KLUTZ** named
Irving Kaputnik.

What girl is going to
remember to lock
the barn door **AFTER**
the **STUD** has **STOLEN**
away?
At a time when the cure for
venereal disease was found,
venereal disease found its way into
more crotches than at any other
time in history.
All because a **KLUTZ** named Roger Kaputnik
reinvented **"THE PILL."**
Only a
KLUTZ
could invent a "pill" that forms
CLOTS.
Some of you men say about VD,
"You're not a real man
until you've had it."
YOU'RE RIGHT!
YOU'VE HAD IT!
YOU'RE NOT A REAL MAN,
YOU'RE STERILE!
For thousands of years
B.P. (Before the Pill)
girls complained,
"ALL MEN ARE ALIKE—
HORNY!"
THEY ONLY WANT ONE THING—
TO OUTJACK THE JACKRABBITS.
So they can barracks-room **BRAG**
about their latest score.
A.P. (After the Pill)
football ceased being
the greatest **CONTACT SPORT**
on campus.

The greatest contact sport became
OPEN DORMS.

During the Middle Ages,
when a couple was arrested
for a particular crime,
the constable would
write on the blotter:
"For **UN-CONNUBIAL KNOWLEDGE.**"
A.P. (After the Pill,)
the girls figured out what the
INITIALS of that crime spelled.
Which is **F   U   C** and that other dirty letter.
Then they proceeded to outjack
the jackrabbits,
so they could dormitory-room **BRAG**
about their latest score.
The **"PILL"** released thousands
of years of inhibited female **HORNINESS.**
It's because they held back
so long—today
they have **MORE STAYING POWER**
than the boys.
As a result,
girls nowadays are saying,
**"ALL MEN ARE ALIKE,
IMPOTENT."**
**THEY ONLY WANT ONE THING,
TO BE LEFT ALONE!"**
The most successful prophylactic
ever invented
was an item called
ABSTINENCE.
That's when **SHE** takes the pill and
uses vaginal jelly—and has a hysterectomy.
HE gets a vasectomy,
puts on a "raincoat,"

**THEN THEY BOTH ABSOLUTELY DON'T DO
ANYTHING SEXUALLY.**
That's **ABSTINENCE.**
Abstinence is the
RAUNCHIEST of all
the **SEX PERVERSIONS.**
The second greatest prophylactic
is a word structure,
"IF YOU CAN'T BE GOOD, BE CAREFUL."
BEING TOO GOOD IS TOO BAD.
Roger Kaputnik, you **KLUTZ,**
you shouldn't have invented a **PILL,**
to make women temporarily sterile,
You should have invented
a pill that made women
PERMANENTLY DOCILE.
**FOR HELL HATH NO FURY
LIKE A WOMAN IN HER
MENSTRUAL CYCLE.**

*　　*　　*　　*

The **TALMUD** tells us,
**"HE WHO SAVES A SINGLE LIFE,
IT IS AS THOUGH HE HAS SAVED
THE ENTIRE WORLD."**

There is a **LIVE BOMB**
circling the sun,
a mis-guided missile
with a **SELF-DESTRUCT MECHANISM.**
The **BOMB** is called **EARTH.**
The **DESTRUCT MECHANISM** is called
PEOPLE.
Instant communications
have shrunk a twenty-five thousand-mile
global girth to a **BEE-BEE PELLET.**
A **BEE-BEE** is also a missile.
Now the **WHOLE PLANET** is being **MUGGED.**
All this is too **TRUE** to be **GOOD.**
And we shout,
**"STOP THE BOMB, I WANT
TO GET OFF."**
And they say,
**"LISTEN, BUSTER, IF YOU CAN'T STAND
THAT HEAT, GET OUT OF THE KITCHEN!"**
BUT THEY WON'T LET US OUT!
The buck stops here,
RIGHT IN OUR GUTS!

Then, to make matters worse,
CHICKEN LITTLE is running around,
like Paul Revere, screaming,
"THE VAN ALLEN BELT IS FALLING!"
AND IT IS.
It's as though someone put up a sign on the world's
door saying: **"PLEASE DISTURB!"**

BUT DON'T PUSH THE PANIC BUTTON!

But what about **THEM,**
the **NUTTY PEOPLE?**
The **NUTS,** like the poor,
we have always had with us,
SINGULAR and **ISOLATED.**
Today, the **NUTS** of the world
are **ORGANIZED** and **POTENT,**
and trying to light the fuse on the
EARTH BOMB.
They say:
**"LET'S GO GATHER NUTS IN MAY
AND SING A GLOBAL SEPTEMBER SONG."**
They are nobodies who are trying
to be somebodies,
even if it means
NO BODIES WILL BE LEFT.
They are trying to be **BIG SHOTS,**
so they **SHOOT PEOPLE.**
They shoot **PRESIDENTS, ATHLETES,
SENATORS, DIPLOMATS, MINISTERS,
LADIES OF HADASSAH BY MAIL,
AND CHILDREN IN SCHOOL BUSSES
BY BAZOOKA.**
ALL NUTS think they are **HEROES.**
ALL NUTS ARE NUTS!
ALL NUTS GIVE NUTS A BAD NAME.
**ALL NUTS ARE GUILTY
UNTIL PROVEN GUILTY.
MOST NUTS GET AWAY WITH IT.**

BUT DON'T PUSH THE PANIC BUTTON!

Nuts skyjack airplanes.
Nuts blow up airplanes.
In the future they plan to skyjack
this **"SPACESHIP CALLED EARTH,"**
AND HOLD IT FOR RANSOM.
So far, **GOD** and the **ISRAELIS** won't pay up.
The future is now.
If these **NUTS** ever get their **NUTTY HANDS**
on **NUTTY ATOMIC WEAPONS,**
then on this live bomb circling the sun
"ALL MEN WILL BE CREMATED EQUAL!"
Never have so few
LOUSED UP
SO MUCH
for **SO MANY.**
The **NUTS** are **LOSERS**
and the **LOSERS ARE WINNING!**

BUT DON'T PUSH THE PANIC BUTTON!
SQUEEZE A NUTCRACKER INSTEAD.

There is an old Arabian tale that tells
of a scorpion and a camel speaking to each other.
The scorpion says, "Hey, you with the humpty-
dumpty back,
back, please take me across the river."
The camel, not knowing he can't talk, answered,
"ARE YOU OUT OF YOUR SAND-PICKING MIND?
IF I DO THAT,
YOU'RE LIABLE TO STING ME AND I'LL DIE."
And the scorpion replied,
"I would be out of my mind if I did that, then
I WOULD DROWN."
This logic made sense to the senseless camel.
So the scorpion mounted the dromedary and the two
creatures became wetbacks crossing the river. While

in the middle of the waters, the scorpion suddenly stung the camel. As the poison spread through the animal's body, he said,

**"YOU NUT. NOW WE'RE BOTH HEADED FOR
     A SIX-FOOT-DEEP
WATERY GRAVE. GIVE ME ONE GOOD REASON WHY
     YOU DID THAT."**

And the gurgling scorpion said, **"THIS IS ARABIA.
WHO NEEDS A GOOD REASON?"**

But it doesn't have to be Arabia, the same story can be told about South America, Ireland, Japan, the U.S. of A., and any other country where they **GROW NUTS.**

BUT DON'T PUSH THE PANIC BUTTON!

Wise was he who said,
**"BLESSED ARE THE MAP MAKERS.
THEY ARE THE ONLY PEOPLE
WHO CAN DRAW NATIONS CLOSE TOGETHER."**

Wise was Zechariah when he said in 14:12,
**"AND THIS SHALL BE THE PLAGUE WHEREWITH
THE LORD WILL SMITE
ALL THE PEOPLE THAT HAVE WARRED
AGAINST JERUSALEM:
THEIR FLESH SHALL CONSUME AWAY WHILE
THEY STAND UPON THEIR FEET,
AND THEIR EYES SHALL CONSUME AWAY
IN THEIR SOCKETS,
AND THEIR TONGUE SHALL CONSUME AWAY
IN THEIR MOUTH."**

What was ol' Zech trying to tell us?
NUCLEAR WAR?
Is blood thicker than water, or is
ARAB OIL BLOODIER

THAN HEAVY WATER IS THICK?
OIL DOES NOT SEEM TO CALM THE WATERS.
BUT IT MIGHT CATCH FIRE AND BURN
THE WHOLE WORLD.
And when the world goes,
who will be around to pay the hijackers,
and who will be around to collect?
NOT THE NUTS.
For what is a man profited, if he shall
gain the whole world and lose his own
SOIL?

The old story tells about a plane flight.
A voice spoke over the plane's intercom.
"This is your captain, the first engine has just gone
        out.
That means we'll be a half hour late in arriving."
A little while later the voice said,
"This is your captain, the second engine is out,
we'll be an hour late in arriving."
The passengers became a little uptight
when another announcement came.
"This is your captain, the third engine
is out, we'll be an hour and a half late."
When the fourth and last engine cut out,
the passengers really became panicky.
One lone passenger called out,
"THIS MEANS WE'LL BE UP HERE ALL NIGHT."

There is a voice calling over the world
intercom:
"THIS IS YOUR CAPTAIN, THE FIRST ENGINE
HAS JUST GONE OUT!"
The question is, who loses a war?
ONLY THOSE PEOPLE WHO ARE KILLED IN ACTION.
In the next **BIG BANG BANG**—that's **EVERYBODY.**

It looks like the world is going to be up there
all night.
ONE NIGHT ONLY.

BUT DON'T PUSH THE PANIC BUTTON.

T'is biblically written of Ishmael, Genesis 16:12:
**"AND HE SHALL BE A WILD ASS OF A MAN:
HIS HAND SHALL BE AGAINST EVERY MAN,
AND EVERY MAN'S HAND AGAINST HIM;"**
Oh, you sons of **ISHMAEL**,
raise your hands already
and make a **PEACE SIGN**.
You have nothing to lose
but your **CHAIN REACTIONS**.
Wisely is it written in the **TALMUD**
that one who shames another in public,
t'is as if he had murdered him.
The nuts of the world are shaming
each other publicly
in murder most foul.
And the **"WHAT ME WORRY"** kid
now **WORRIES**.

BUT DON'T PUSH THE PANIC BUTTON!

These **NUTS** are not lovable.
Yet the ancient **HEBREWS** taught us to
"LOVE THY NEIGHBOR."
THAT some neighbors **CAN DO**.
Rabbi Joshua Ben Joseph taught us to
LOVE THY ENEMY."
THAT PRACTICALLY NO ONE CAN DO.

NOW YOU CAN PUSH THE PANIC BUTTON!

That's **THEM**, the **NUTS**.
But what about **US**—
THE SEMI-NUTS?
We've already got our semi-nutty hands
on **NUTTY ATOMIC WEAPONS**.
We can **SEMI-BLOW UP** this rounded world
to a **FLAT DISK**.
Then we would **ALL FALL OFF THE EDGE**.
Gravity keeps the world
RIGHT SIDE UP
when the world is **UPSIDE DOWN**.

The good Rabbi said, **"LOVE THY ENEMY."**
But he was a **SUPERJEW**.
The rest of us are only **SEMIS**.
So we'll have to **SEMI-LOVE OUR ENEMIES**.
WE GOTTA!
OR WE GOT NOTHING!
So we quote,
"ASSUME A VIRTUE IF YOU HAVE IT NOT."
We can assume a **PHONY STATUS SYMBOL**,
when we can **AFFORD IT NOT**,
then why not a virtue?
That means being totally sincere—
WHETHER WE MEAN IT OR NOT.
If we can't **LOVE 'EM**,
then **LIKE 'EM**.
If we can't **LIKE 'EM**,
then we can **HATE THEIR GUTS**,
but **LIKE THEIR LIVERS**,
and **FEED THEIR STOMACHS**,
if you can't do these things
then we'll just **LEAVE THEM TO HELL ALONE**.
THAT'LL make them **LIKE US**.
So many groups based their ideal
on the **BROTHERHOOD OF MAN**,

yet refused to be their **BROTHERS' KEEPER**
or their **BROTHERS' BROTHER.**
Flower children said they **LOVED EVERYBODY**
EXCEPT
THE FUZZ, THE PENTAGON and their **PARENTS.**
OTHER BROTHERLY LOVERS SAID,
"I hate **BIGOTS** and **NIGGERS!**"
THE BIGOT THEY ARE, THE HARDER
THEY SQUALL!

KEEP YOUR FINGER ON THE PANIC BUTTON!

Amongst us **SEMI-NUTS**
there are some rare, totally noble beings,
like Dr. Roger Kessler, who once said
to an eminent golfer,
"Your greatest pleasure is getting
A HOLE IN ONE,
MY GREATEST PLEASURE
is sticking my finger up a rectum
and **NOT FINDING A LUMP.**"

And there are those who make their
words **SWEET** and **TENDER,**
for tomorrow they may have to
EAT THEM.

The twice-told tale tells of
a Rabbi admonishing a member
of his congregation.
"Look out the window,"
said the learned cleric.
"WHAT DO YOU SEE?"
"People," says the congregant.
"Now look into the mirror. What
do you see?"
"Myself."

63

"**AH HA**," says the wise leader.
"You look through a pane of glass
and you see **PEOPLE**.
Add a little **SILVER** behind the glass
and you see only **YOURSELF**."
So to save the world, **SMASH
ALL MIRRORS**.
So you say, "What good would
that do? It will only bring
SEVEN YEARS OF BAD LUCK."
Not to the **NINETY-YEAR OLDS**,
they'd have a guarantee of
SEVEN MORE YEARS.

Humor is often based on
UNHAPPINESS.
If we eliminated **HUMOR**,
maybe the world would be
HAPPY AGAIN.

The question is,
WHAT THE HELL IS HELL?
Some say it's a long dining room table,
stacked with the most scrumptious,
finger-licking good food.
The people who are damned
are seated facing each other
and **STARVING: WHY?**
Their elbows are stiff, and they can't
feed themselves.
However, they could feed each other
across the table.
But they are so mean and **SELFISH**,
they can't see the solution.
In that place of **FIRE AND BRIMSTONE**
it's **NOT** the **HEAT**, it's the **STUPIDITY**.

So, if we can't love our enemies,
PUSH FOOD IN THEIR FACES.
That is not **TRUE BROTHERHOOD
OF MAN.**
We may never have that.
There cannot be **BROTHERHOOD,**
as long as
the **MASOCHIST** says,
"BEAT ME!"
and the **SADIST** says,
"NO!"
As long as the **LAST COMMANDMENT**
is the **FIRST** one we break.
"THOU SHALT NOT COVET."
And we say,
"There isn't a jealous bone
in my body."
And there isn't
IT'S ALL IN THE MIND.
So how do we **DEFUSE** this **LIVE BOMB**
called **EARTH?**
NOT WITH BROTHERLY LOVE.
THAT HAS FAILED BECAUSE OF SELFISHNESS.
And yet it is with
TOTAL SELF-CENTERED SELFISHNESS
that we'll find the **SOLUTION.**
The ancient **TALMUDIC** wisdom declares:
**"HE WHO SAVES A SINGLE LIFE,
IT IS AS THOUGH HE SAVED
THE ENTIRE WORLD."**
That is an anachronism.
**TODAY,
YOU HAVE TO SAVE
THE ENTIRE WORLD
IN ORDER TO SAVE A SINGLE LIFE,
YOUR OWN!**

If **EVERYONE** acted that **SELFISHLY COLLECTIVELY**,
feeding their enemies across the table
in order to save themselves,
that would be **TOTAL SELFISHNESS**.
And the **WORLD BOMB** would be
DEFUSED with a **BURP—**
not with a **BANG**.
And the only **BANG**
that will be heard will come
from some **CHILD ROGER**, who shall lead us
and have the compassion to say,
while playing war,
**"BANG! BANG! YOU'RE
NOT
DEAD!"**
The world does not owe **US** a living.
WE owe the world
LIFE.
If you don't believe in **MIRACLES**
then you're not **REALISTIC**.

**NOW YOU CAN TAKE YOUR HAND OFF
THE PANIC BUTTON.**

*   *   *   *

SEX IS A FOUR LETTERED WORD

Ever since men began to change history
by writing history books,
men also searched for the
PERFECT APHRODISIAC, a sexual stimulant.
Men tried potions mixed with the
wart of frogs,
ailerons of bat's wing,
the powdered horn of a rhinoceros,
the lint of a Gypsy's navel,
and the fly of the Spanish.
None worked.
It wasn't until the late twentieth century
that men finally discovered
the **PERFECT APHRODISIAC**
to sexually stimulate them.
It was a secret ingredient called—
WOMEN.

*   *   *   *

Bigotry is based on fear.
Fear leads to hate.
Hate is based on basics.
Basic is **SEX.**
So when a white man
hates a black man,
it's because he fears
that the black man
has a **LARGER SEX ORGAN**
than his.
Black is a color,
not a length.
So if a white man
feels inferior sexually
to a black man,
all he has to do is
paint his organ **BASIC BLACK.**

Jewish men have always had
a reputation for being the
best husbands.
So many non-Jewish girls
have sought Jewish husbands,
because they were
better family men
and better providers.
So non-Jewish men became bigoted,
fearful and hateful, based on
BASIC SEX.
They figured Jewish husbands
provided better **SEX ORGANS.**
So they made it a **CRIME**
punishable by **DEATH**
for a Jewish man to marry
a non-Jewish girl.

All they had to do was
paint their non-Jewish organs
BLUE and **WHITE** with a
STAR OF DAVID on them.
This would not provide
a **BETTER SEX ORGAN** for the gals.
But it would guarantee
that in a **YMHA** locker room,
such a sight would bring
at least one chorus of
HATIKVAH,
the Hebrew National Anthem.

According to Dr. Reuben,
the **BIGGEST SEX ORGAN**
is the **GRAY MATTER**
called the **BRAIN**.
So if you have to paint
that other sex organ
a different color —
try **BATTLESHIP GRAY**.

*   *   *   *

In the ancient Hebraic book
called the **MIDRASH**, it is written:
"**AN ADULTEROUS WOMAN IN HER
LOVER'S APARTMENT SWEARS ON
HER HUSBAND'S LIFE.**"
Even then they had the
UNORIGINAL SIN.

*   *   *   *

In many cultures the slang expression
for the male sex organ usually denotes
A BAD PERSON.
In **YIDDISH** the slang expression
for the male sex organ denotes
A FOOLISH PERSON.
Therefore we might assume that
many cultures prudishly consider
SEX as **BAD.**
While amongst the Hebrews,
it might be considered
FOOLISH—
but **BAD** it's not.
In actuality, the Hebrews consider
SEX SACRED.
That Yiddish word cannot be repeated here
because to some people it's
a **DIRTY WORD.**
While words like **WAR** and **VIOLENCE**
are **CLEAN WORDS.**
If by chance you do not know what that
Yiddish word is,
then you are a **SCHMUCK.**

*   *   *   *

Statistics show that
very few **JEWISH WOMEN**
get the dangerous disease of the **CERVIX.**
Doctors theorize that it has
something to do with their
CIRCUMCISED MATES.
Women also theorize that
CIRCUMCISED MEN make
BETTER LOVERS.
Therefore it is theorized
that this ancient Hebrew
practice of **CIRCUMCISION** is
THE KINDEST CUT OF ALL.

* * * *

Now that pornography is
so prevalent,
the **LITERACY RATE** might go up.
PORNOGRAPHY is in the crotch
of the beholder.

* * * *

A swinger does not play
musical beds to satisfy his
urge.
He swings to satisfy his ego.
So he's not a swinger,
he's a score keeper.
That's why it's called
SCORING.

Today they are **DOING IT MORE
BUT ENJOYING IT LESS.**

* * * *

The question is asked,
"Where do all the dirty jokes come from."
Some authorities say they originate in prisons,
where people are confined, unhappy, frightened,
disturbed, and deprived.
It would seem that people do not
JOKE about things when they are **HAPPY.**
Psychologists tell me that people who do
not make their homes in prisons and are
preoccupied with telling dirty stories are
usually themselves impotent and sexually
inadequate.
The psychologists must be right, because
**I CAN'T THINK OF ANY DIRTY STORIES
TO GIVE YOU AS AN EXAMPLE.**

*   *   *   *

Roger Kaputnik writes to his kin:

"My darling daughter Nancy,
I am a **MALE CHAUVINIST!**
Whatever **GOD** made me, **I LIKE.**
Be you a **FEMALE CHAUVINIST.**
Whatever **GOD** made you, **LOVE!**
So you are studying about **WOMEN'S LIBERATION.**
GOOD!
Of those who teach you, **WATCH!**
Do they like themselves **LESS,**
and of men, **HATE MORE?**
Then they are not teachers,
they are **UNLEARNERS.**
Of them, **BEWARE!**
Of those who say,
**'STARVE A RAT TODAY, DON'T FEED YOUR
          HUSBAND!'**
—LOOK ASKANCE!
Only **RATS** marry **RATS.**
Of those who say,
**'FEED A TIGER TODAY, FOR HE COMETH FROM
          THE
CONCRETE JUNGLE AND WEARY IS THE HUNTER!'**
HARKEN!
Only **TIGERS** marry **TIGRESSES.**
Of those who teach equality and coexistence,
LISTEN!
Of those who teach **SHE** and **SHE, DEAFEN!**
Of those who teach **SHE** and **HE, ABSORB**!
What I just wrote, **I LIKE!**
Whatever you write, **LOVE!**
LOVE is a good way to end these ramblings.
                    LOVE,
                    BIG DADDY"

So the **WOMEN'S LIBBERS** did a lot of
HOLLERING to be just as **LIBERATED**
and just as **EQUAL** as the
MALE CHAUVINIST SEXIST PIGS.
Not just **LIBERATED,** but **MORE LIBERATED.**
Not just **EQUAL,** but **MORE EQUAL.**
So they **HOLLERED** for:
**SEXUAL FREEDOM, THE NEW MORALITY,
CONTRACEPTIVES, AND ABORTION ON DEMAND.**
Those women who backed the **HOLLERING**
WOMEN'S LIBBERS wished to be
FEMALE CHAUVINIST SEXIST PIGGY BACKERS.

Some of us old-fashioned Roger Kaputnik-
type male chauvinist sexist pigs
believe that
WOMEN'S PLACE IS IN THE KITCHEN—
if they happen to choose **THAT** uncomfortable
place to be **SEXUALLY LIBERATED.**

For doing all that **HOLLERING**
the **WOMEN'S LIBBERS** got many things:
**HOARSE VOICES,
SEX ON DEMAND,
UNWANTED PREGNANCIES ON DEMAND,
UNWANTED ABORTIONS ON DEMAND,
UNWANTED SYPHILIS ON DEMAND,**
and all those other **UNEQUAL
UNLIBERATING BURDENS THAT
ONLY HOLLERING WOMEN MUST BEAR.**

So the **ONLY ONES** who **REALLY** got
SEXUAL FREEDOM in this **NEW MORALITY**
were the **UNENCUMBERED
MALE CHAUVINIST SEXIST PIGS.**
And they didn't even have to
HOLLER to get it.
76

Males also need **LIBERATION.**
As long as grandmothers, mothers, and wives
tell their Roger Kaputnik-type men
**THAT THEY MUST BE MAN ENOUGH
TO MAKE A LIVING.
THAT THEY MUST BE MAN ENOUGH
TO BE A BIG SUCCESS.
THAT THEY MUST BE MAN ENOUGH
TO FIGHT WARS.
THAT THEY MUST BE MAN ENOUGH
TO BE TOUGH AT ALL TIMES.**
And when it comes time
for Roger to stand up against
his pushy women—
ROGER IS NOT MAN ENOUGH.

*　　*　　*　　*

Humor often depends on a point
of view as from where you're
standing.
I was talking to a Women's Libber
who was writing an article for a
women's magazine.
She was furious as she related
something she had discovered that
Freud had written.
He said something to this effect:
"Those who control fire
control civilization.
A man can urinate on a fire
and put it out.
A woman couldn't do that,
therefore **MAN IS SUPERIOR."**
I laughed,
SHE DIDN'T.
From where **SHE** was standing,
it wasn't funny.
**SHE WAS STANDING OVER THE FIRE,
AND COULDN'T PUT IT OUT.**

*   *   *   *

Those of **WOMEN'S LIB** persuasion
claim that the **OLD-TIME RELIGION**
did not treat them fairly.
This is a **HALF-TRUTH**,
and a half-truth, in spite of what some say,
IS NOT A WHOLE LIE,
any more than a **WHOLE LIE** is a **HALF-TRUTH**.
In Yiddish there is a word **BALEBOSS**.
It means the **MALE CHAUVINIST BOSS**.
There is another Yiddish word **BALEBOSSTEH**.
It means the **FEMALE BOSS** of the house.
At a hasty look it might seem that the
Orthodox Jewish Culture was **ANTI-FEMALE**.
She had to sit separate in the synagogue,
while her male chauvinist husband said prayers like
**"THANK YOU, GOD, FOR NOT MAKING ME A
        WOMAN."**
With a more studied look you will find that
amongst the Orthodox and Hasidic groups,
the male chauvinist sat all day studying
in the synagogue—
   while his **"UNLIBERATED"** wife **RAN THE BUSINESS,
THE CHILDREN, THE HOUSE, AND HER
MALE CHAUVINIST HUSBAND.**
So you see who really was the **BALEBOSS**—
It was the **BALEBOSSTEH.**
CHESS originated in Asia.
It became a Jewish game when
a couple of Hebes named Fischer and Spassky
became champs of the world.
The name **CHESS** comes from the Persian
male chauvinist word **SHAH**, meaning **KING**.
Yet in the game itself, the **KING** is **LIMITED**
in his moves,
**WHILE THE QUEEN IS TOTALLY LIBERATED.
SHE CAN MOVE FREELY IN ALL DIRECTIONS.**
In other words she is the **BALEBOSSTEH.**

Ancient Israel was called
"THE LAND OF MILK AND HONEY."
The **MILK** comes from the **BALEBOSSTEH**
of these animals of the **BOVINE** persuasion.
To this day a cow is called **"BOSSY."**
Amongst the **HONEY MAKERS** it is
the **QUEEN BEE** who is **KING**—
or the **BALEBOSSTEH.**

So if a woman really wants to become **LIBERATED,**
she can hope in the next life she comes back as
A JEWISH MOTHER
or a **CHESS PIECE,**
or a **COW.**
then she'll **BE** the **BALEBOSSTEH.**

*   *   *   *

© 1965 by E. C. Publications, Inc.

Geologists tell that the mountains
in New York City consist of
strata of concrete, steel, glass,
and bad taste.
They are called office buildings.
Our hero Roger worked in one
such office.
His work was incidental to his real
profession, which was being a
professional observer—
a **YENTA** (Yiddish version of noseybody).
Roger observed that the firm
across the street worked only
half a day on Saturdays.
Roger could plainly see that after
the others had left, one swinger
and secretary stayed behind
to break things—
like the **SEVENTH COMMANDMENT.**
He could see all this **HANKY-PANKY**
through the glass window
on which was lettered the firm's name.
So Roger dialed that number.
The swinger and swingee had only
gotten around to **HANKYING,**
when the phone disturbed them.
The swinger picked up the phone
and Roger said in a deep voice,
**"THIS IS GOD, YOU OUGHT TO BE
ASHAMED OF YOURSELF."**
They never got around to **PANKYING.**

*   *   *   *

STAND ON YOUR OWN
TWO CLOVEN HOOVES

The generation of the late sixties
and early seventies was nicknamed
"THE WOODSTOCK GENERATION."
Why? Because supposedly the first big Rock
Festival was held there.
Actually it took place a few miles away
in a town called **BETHEL**, New York.
BETHEL means **HOUSE OF GOD.**
During the Festival **GOD** was not in **HIS** house.
The noise of the loudspeakers and the
acrid smell of pot drove **HIM** out.
So **HE** went to Woodstock for the weekend.
So why was the Festival called Woodstock?
The P.R. man didn't want anybody to know
that they played to an **EMPTY HOUSE.**
Nobody wants it kicked around that
GOD IS NOT WITH THEM.
So the generation was named
for the place where **GOD WAS.**

*   *   *   *

The **WOODSTOCK GENERATION** did not
invent **DESPAIR,**
but they developed it into a new art
form called **CREATIVE DESTRUCTION.**
Runaways ran away from despair
TO despair.
It became an **"IN THING"** to be
down and out.
The kids took "downers" to feel
DOWNER.
To them, **"ONE OF THOSE DAYS"** was **EVERYDAY.**
To them, in the game of living, the odds were
they **LOSE A FEW** and **LOSE A FEW.**
It was as if they made a great
new discovery, that
"PAIN HURTS."
And it felt good not to feel good.
Of despair, the Hebrew writers wrote
and wrote and wrote.
The Catholics later summed it all up very well
when they considered
"THE SIN OF DESPAIR"
ONE OF THE WORST SINS—
It is as if the **DESPONDENT ONE**
has **GIVEN UP** on **GOD'S ABILITY**
TO HANDLE THE SITUATION.
Of despair I would like to write
and write and write—
but it **DEPRESSES ME.**
So **I LEAVE IT TO GOD.**
Let **HIM** handle the situation
by putting a Band-Aid on
the whole **WOODSTOCK GENERATION.**
And save a couple of Band-Aids
for their despondent parents.

*　　　*　　　*　　　*

Naches is a Yiddish word
for pride of children.
Therefore when the mid-
nineteen sixties and seventies
produced the most loused-up children
that ever were,
and your kids aren't quite as
bad as the others—
THAT'S NACHES.

So you see, it's really not such a
BAD GENERATION. At least it's mobile.
50 percent are in **NEUTRAL**.
25 percent are in **REVERSE**.
23 percent are in **DRIVE**,
but without a steering wheel,
2 percent are in **DRIVE**
WITH a steering wheel,
but they are crashing into
the other 98 percent.

American kids today
don't cut the umbilical cord
until their teens.
Then they use it
TO STRANGLE THEIR PARENTS.

*   *   *   *

It is written that the **MESSIAH**
comes when a generation comes
that is either **ALL GOOD**
or **ALL BAD**.
GOOD IT'S NOT.
Prepare for the **MESSIANIC AGE**.

*   *   *   *

When we were more primitive
than we are now,
WE LET IT ALL HANG OUT.
If someone hassled our forebears
they uninhibitedly gave the hassler
A MOUTHFUL OF KNUCKLES
letting his dentures **HANG OUT.**
As we became less primitive
we became more **INHIBITED.**
Now when we are hassled,
WE LET IT ALL HANG IN.
This has formed **HANG-UPS, ULCERS,
ANXIETY NEUROSES,** and our dollars
shrunk to the shrink.
The kids looked at their parents and said,
"YEECCH!"
So the kids of today invented
a whole new philosophy of living,
**"DOWN WITH INHIBITIONS.
LET IT ALL HANG OUT."**
Now they don't suffer from
HANG-UPS, ulcers, or anxiety neuroses—
just **SYPHILIS** from **UNINHIBITED SEX,
SCRAMBLED BRAINS** from **UNINHIBITED DRUGS,
SCLEROSIS** of the **LIVER** from **UNINHIBITED
         DRINKING,
CHROMOSOME DAMAGE** from **UNINHIBITED LSD**
and an assorted variety of other niceties
which will lead to
INHIBITING HANG-UPS
worse than anything their parents ever had.
And **THEIR CHILDREN** will say,
"YEECCH!"

*   *   *   *

In a world of so many **BODIES**
EVERYBODY feels like a **NOBODY**.
So we all wear some kind of **LABEL**
saying, **"HEY, LOOK AT ME, I'M A SOMEBODY."**
There are those who wear the label
**"I AM DESCENDED FROM THE LATE,
GREAT SO-AND-SO."**
Like potatoes, the best part of them is
UNDERGROUND.
The car freak wears a label that says,
**"I'M A BIG NOTHING, BUT I DRIVE
A BIG SOMETHING."**
There was once a theatrical person
who had only **SIX** people show up
at one of her performances.
She put on a label that said,
"Anyway, **SEVEN** showed up."
Then there is the old-lady status-seeker,
who wears the label that says,
"I'VE GOT MORE TROUBLES THAN YOU DO."
Down at the bottom of the list of
label-wearers is the kind called
"LABEL-LOOKERS."
In a generation that produced the most
ANTIMATERIALISTIC KIDS,
it has also produced the most
MATERIALISTIC FEMALE BRATS.
They buy the most expensive apparel
not because they have good taste,
but because they have the **BAD TASTE**
to say,
"LOOK WHAT I GOT, AND YOU HAVEN'T."
Then they take off the expensive apparel
in the boys' dorm and say,
"LOOK WHAT I GOT AND YOU HAVEN'T."
That's the label they wear
when they don't wear.

No matter how tattered their jeans be,
no matter how many patches there are
where there are no holes,
and holes where there are no patches—
it matters not.
All that matters to a **LABEL-LOOKER**
is that the **LABEL** read
"SAKS FIFTH AVENUE" or **"BONWIT TELLER."**
THAT makes the **SLOB** a **PRINCESS.**
And the immaculately dressed girl
whose label reads **"WOOLWORTH,"**
they say **SHE'S** a **SLOB**.

If you think I'm talking about you,
I'm not.
But try the expensive shoe on for size.
If it **HURTS,**
then it probably **FITS.**

I overheard one such **LABEL-LOOKING SENIOR**
giving advice to a freshman.
"If you want to make it in this school,
 DON'T BE CAUGHT DEAD IN A PINTO OR MAVERICK.
BUT IT'S OKAY TO BE CAUGHT DEAD IN A
CORVETTE.
THEN YOU'LL MAKE IT."

At another school, there was this
SORORITY made up of only **LABEL-LOOKERS.**
During the rush, a freshman named Regina
was being examined, whether she was worthy.
The **LABEL-LOOKERS** graciously helped Regina
off with her coat.
While Regina was being interrogated in
one room,

the other **LABEL-LOOKERS** were looking at the
label on her coat.
The **LABEL-LOOKERS** came in to announce that
Regina **DID NOT QUALIFY**
because her label read, **"ROBERT GALL,"**
a **LOW-PRICED CHAIN STORE**.
Regina announced that all her clothes
had the same label because her father
OWNED THAT CHAIN OF LOW-PRICED STORES.
The **LABEL-LOOKERS** were stunned,
as if struck by a **PLAIN PIPE RACK.**
They should have quit while
they were still **BEHIND**.

This story is true.
Only the label **"ROBERT GALL"**
is fictitious.

*   *   *   *

So you're this little kid-type person.
And they give you all these toys
to play with—
toy fire engines, toy trucks, toy campers,
toy sports cars, and toy moving vans.
With all these toys you say you're
NOT HAPPY.
That's because in order to be
a kid-type person today,
you have to be a member of
THE TEAMSTERS UNION.
And you can't cough up the dues.

So you're this teenage-type person.
Your father reads in the Bible:
"SPARE THE ROD AND SPOIL THE CHILD."
So when you're obnoxious,
your father takes the rod—
and **DOESN'T KNOW WHAT TO DO WITH IT.**

and you use all the four-letter
Anglo-Saxon dirty words.
And your mother says,
**"EVEN YOUR FATHER DOESN'T
USE SUCH LANGUAGE."**
And you say,
**"HE WAS ONLY A SERGEANT IN
THE ARMY. I'M A TEEN-AGE-TYPE
PERSON."**
But you're not **HAPPY.**
Because children should be
OBSCENE BUT NOT HEARD.

So you're this young adult-type person.
And you're not happy.
You want and want and want.
You even want to go back to being
a little kid-type person, when
you almost made the **TEAMSTERS UNION.**
The founding papas in their
Declaration of Independence
DID NOT ASK FOR HAPPINESS —
only **THE PURSUIT** thereof.
When a dog chases a car
he's having a **HOWLING GOOD TIME.**
What if he should **CATCH IT?**
Does he drag it off and bury it
like a bone?
No, he's **DISAPPOINTED,**
and looks around for another car
to **CHASE.**
So **HAPPINESS** is only the **PURSUIT.**
Like a dog, you are
PURSUING CARS.
You want a **CORVETTE,** a **MACH 1,**
a **LOMBORGHINI**
But you can't always get it.
So you **SHOULD BE VERY HAPPY.**

*   *   *   *

The old joke tells about a man
who comes home unexpectedly
and finds someone else
consummating his marriage.
In a rage, he pulls out a gun
and puts it to his temple.
His wife screams at him,
**"ARE YOU CRAZY? YOU'RE GOING
TO SHOOT YOURSELF."**
And he says,
**"YES, I AM.
FIRST ME,
THEN YOU!"**

There were some young fascists
of the New Left going around saying,
"KILL YOUR PARENTS."
And the young **SCHMUCKY** followers
said to their parents,
**"FIRST ME,
THEN YOU!"**
All too often it happened
just that way.

*   *   *   *

Roger Kaputmouth once said to Mr. Mead E. Ochre,
"As long as some blacks who try to make it
are called,
'OREO COOKIES (black on the outside, white
on the inside)'** by other blacks
then we'll have **MEDIOCRITY.**
As long as some blacks who try to make it
are called,
'UNCLE TOMS'
by other blacks,
then we'll have **MEDIOCRITY.**
As long as some Indians who try to make it
are called
'UNCLE TOM TOMS'
by other Indians,
then we'll have **MEDIOCRITY.**
As long as some Jews who try to make it
are called,
'PUSHY'
by non-Jews,
then we'll have **MEDIOCRITY.**
As long as the Third World Conference
accomplishes nothing but the
CONDEMNATION OF ISRAEL
for trying to make it,
then we'll have **MEDIOCRITY.**

As long as we go on calling names,
and putting down people who try
to work in the **MERIT SYSTEM,**
we'll have **MEDIOCRITY.**
These words went into one ear of
Mr. Mead E. Ochre, and out his mouth
loudly saying,
"AH SHADDAP, YOU DAMN EGGHEAD."

* * * *

In nineteen hundred and yesterday,
Charlie Dickens wrote about the
French Revolution in the book
called *A TALE OF TWO CITIES*.
His opening paragraph said it
was the **BEST OF TIMES** and
the **WORST OF TIMES**.
Charlie could have written the
same thing about **TODAY**.
MODERN TECHNOLOGY with its
MASS MANUFACTURING and
MACH 1 TRANSPORTATION
has exhausted itself with **EXHAUST**,
adding a **FILTH DIMENSION**
to our **THREE-DIMENSIONAL EXISTENCE**.
With all the modern conveniences,
we also have the modern **INCONVENIENCES** . . .
PAYING FOR THE MODERN CONVENIENCES.
So these are the **WORST OF TIMES**.
BUT, it's also the **BEST OF TIMES**.
We can count our blessings on
ONE FINGER.
That finger pushes a button
that gives us instant transistorized
MUSIC.
Next to **SEX, MUSIC** is the most
ECSTATIC HUMAN EXPERIENCE.
MUSIC next to **SEX** helps with
the **RHYTHM METHOD**.
In the yesterday, only the
mightiest emperor could have
music at his beck and call.
Beck played the **HARP**.
In the today, sex has new packaging.
Movies have become Xed,
and magazines kinkied.

But sex has still remained the same,
except now we have become
VOYEURS instead of **ENJOYERS**.
Music also has new packaging.
The American **KNOW-HOW**
has become **AMERICAN KNOW-WHO**.
The **WHO** is cheap Japanese labor.
Japanese mass-produced electronics
have saturated Pearl Harbor,
strafed Scranton, shaken Shaker Heights,
scarred Scarsdale, and made Woodstock
a laughing stock for adults.
Printed circuits have put **MUSIC**
at **EVERYBODY'S** beck and call.
Today Beck plays
the **ELECTRIC GUITAR.**
In the today, any kid with a
minimum of money mooched from Mama,
has rings on his fingers, bells on
his toes, and **HE SHALL HAVE MUSIC
WHEREVER HE GOES—**
AMed, **FM**ed, **HI-FI**ed, **STEREO**ed, **QUADROPHONIC**ed,
CASSETTEDed, **EIGHT-TRACK**ed, **PHONOGRAPH**ed,
and to Mama
EARitated.
The portable radio on a kid's shoulder
is technology's new
SECURITY BLANKET.
The richest king living in the highest
high-rise, high-rental palace
was a welfare case compared to
any kid living in a
graffiti-smeared low-rent
basement apartment.
No past king knew the ecstasy
of **STEREOPHONIC EARPHONES.**

The kid wearing these
ELECTRONIC EARMUFFS
has **LOUD ECSTATIC MUSIC**
vibrating through his **WHOLE BODY.**
EVERY VITAL ORGAN becomes an **EAR.**
And that's why he dances like
he has an **EARACHE** in his **FEET.**
He plays it so aggravatingly **LOUD**
to kill the pain of **GROWING UP.**
This makes music a pain killer
to the kid.
For the same reason he takes **NARCOTICS.**
The kid doesn't want to grow up like
his father.
BUT HE WILL.
So this **FILTH DIMENSION** we live in
has some anesthetizing ingredients.
The technology of **CARS**
has replaced **WALKING.**
TV has replaced **SEEING.**
COMPUTERS have replaced **THINKING.**
This makes **TECHNOLOGY**
a **TECHNICAL ERROR.**
But the **TECHNOLOGY** of **INSTANT MUSIC**
has **NOT** replaced **LISTENING.**
Wallow in the **TREBLE.**
Rub the **BASS** in your pores.
Because **CANNED MUSIC IS ABOUT THE ONLY
        THING**
we've got **GOING FOR US** to make this
the **BEST OF TIMES.**

*   *   *   *

George Bernard Shaw said something
to the effect that,
"Youth is such a wonderful thing, it's a shame to
waste it on young people."
George blew it.
It was a shame to waste such
a **CLEVER REMARK** on them.
The young people of the mid-sixties
wasted their time being against
the **ESTABLISHMENT** and the
"PROTESTANT WORK ETHIC."
"WORK" became a four-lettered **DIRTY WORD.**
Simply put, the **PROTESTANT ETHIC** is
"HARD WORK, GOD AND COUNTRY,"
which is neither **SIMPLE**
nor **PROTESTANT.**
It's **COMPLICATED** and **JEWISH.**
During an adult college course, while tracing the
supposed **ETHIC** to the New England Puritans,
        one student said:
"I work for one of these **WASPS** who is a descendent
from that stock. He works very hard, long hours, he
lives below his means, he attends religious services
regularly, and he is very patriotic."
Another student added,
"I have such a boss also. Except that he's **JEWISH.**"
If **WASP** is an abbreviation of
WHITE ANGLO-SAXON PROTESTANTS
then **JEWISH** must be an abbreviation of
**JEHOVAH ENCOURAGING WASPS IMITATING -
        STALWART HEBREWS.**
Of hard work, the **OLD TESTAMENT** says
that when Adam and Eve **GOOFED** while **GOOFING**
        off in Paradise,
GOD threw them out and said that henceforth
they'd have to "work by the sweat of their brow."

Of **GOD,** the **OLD TESTAMENT** says and says and
    says.
Of **COUNTRY,** it says:
"PROCLAIM LIBERTY THROUGHOUT THE LAND."
There is a ding-dong in Philadelphia
that busted a gut making that proclamation.
The word **SABBATH** comes from the Hebrew word
SHABBAS, meaning the seventh day.
From which we get the word **SABBATICAL,**
meaning the **SEVENTH YEAR.**
From which we get one do-nothing year off,
from which we get ants in the pants,
from which we get the expression
"THE SEVEN-YEAR ITCH."
The Puritans strictly observed the Sabbath.
History tells us they listed many infractions of the
Sabbath laws.
Such as:
Not hiring out a horse, not taking a long journey,
not driving a cart, not shelling corn, not fiddling
or drawing and not swearing.
After all those **NOTS,** swearing was needed.
From all these Puritan Sabbath laws we
see they didn't borrow from the Jews—
they **STOLE** it. Which is breaking another
JEWISH LAW,
"THOU SHALT NOT STEAL."
There is one difference.
"THE PROTESTANT ETHIC" be changed to the
"YOU ARE BORN A SINNER."
The **JEWISH ETHIC** believes
"YOU are born **INNOCENT,"**
THEN you become a **SINNER.**
We do owe the good Pilgrims a **THANKS**
for giving us the holiday called
"THANKSGIVING."

They gave it to us after
the **HEBREWS** gave it to us
several thousand years earlier.
The **HEBREWS** called it
"SUCCOTH" or
"THE FEAST OF THE TABERNACLE,"
or
"THANKS TO GOD FOR GIVING US ROAST TURKEY."
Oh yes, we got that from the **HEBREWS** also,
only they spelled it differently,
B-O-I-L-E-D C-H-I-C-K-E-N.

The Puritans wore long hair, which was considered
acceptable on the head of
upper-class Puritans like Cromwell and Winthrop.
But on the head of a lower-class person,
they considered long hair a sign of **VANITY.**
Today they would call a long-haired person
"A DIRTY HIPPIE."
The Puritans were keenly concerned about a
"GOOD BARGAIN."
Today they call it
"JEWING HIM DOWN."
In the yesteryears it was called,
"YANKEE-ING HIM UP."
In the chronicles of the Puritans
it briefly mentions that a Jew
visited the colony one day.
He was told to scram before nightfall.
The Puritans were afraid that the
Jew might influence them in his ways.
They already were influenced before he
got there.
In no way am I proposing that the expression
"THE PROTESTANT ETHIC" be changed to the
      "JEWISH ETHIC."

**JEWS ARE DAMNED ENOUGH FOR THE
GOOD THINGS THEY GAVE TO THE WORLD.**
So if the young people were against the
WORK ETHIC.
they were not against the established **PROTESTANTS,**
they were against the
JEWISH WORK ETHIC.
The Jews are **NOT** the "**ESTABLISHMENT.**"
So this makes it **ANTI-SEMITISM.**
But there is no such thing as anti-Semitism.
THERE IS ONLY GOD THE FATHER,
who has **MANY CHILDREN,**
of whom **HE** has chosen the Jews
as his favorite.
Therefore there is no anti-Semitism,
**BUT THERE IS A HECK OF A LOT OF
SIBLING RIVALRY.**

*   *   *   *

THE JOY OF BEING YIDDISH

WITH GRATEFUL ACKNOWLEDGMENT TO MY GOOD FRIEND AL JAFFEE.

*   *   *   *

**A ROGER KAPUTNIK ISN'T ALWAYS
JEWISH.
EVEN WHEN HE'S JEWISH
HE ISN'T ALWAYS JEWISH.**
Since Hebraic law reasons:
You always know who the **MOTHER IS**
As for the **FATHER—**
"VER VASTE" (WHO KNOWS).
So every Jew in the world
is only **HALF JEWISH**
and **HALF VER VASTE.**
Except for **US** Roger Kaputniks.
OUR mothers don't know
WHO *WE* **ARE.**

*   *   *   *

Jewish humor is a cry for help which
comes out in the form of a stifled laugh,
which makes the hearer do the shrieking
and relieves the teller.
So we hear this kind of departing cry for
help from one Jew to another,
"I'LL SEE YOU TUESDAY,
IF I LIVE.
IF NOT, I'LL SEE YOU WEDNESDAY."

During World War II, this was a common cry,
"HITLER SHOULD LOSE ALL HIS TEETH
EXCEPT ONE—
SO HE COULD HAVE A TOOTHACHE."

Another example tells this fictitious story:
Hitler was walking down the streets of Berlin
when he spied a Jew. Pulling out his revolver,
Hitler shouted,
"JUDE, EAT THE MUD IN THE STREET."
The frightened Jew fell on all fours
and began to do so. This made Hitler
laugh so hard that he dropped the gun.
The Jew quickly picked up the gun and said,
"OKAY, WISE GUY, NOW YOU GET ON ALL FOURS
AND EAT THE MUD IN THE STREET."
The frightened Hitler began to do so.
But the Jew lost his nerve, dropped the gun
and ran home. On reaching his house,
he cried out to his wife,
"BECKY, BECKY, YOU'LL NEVER GUESS
WHO I JUST HAD LUNCH WITH."

*　　*　　*　　*

*   *   *   *

In interviewing the former Chief Rabbi of Ireland,
he told me that there is an organization of
Irish Catholics who believe that **THEY**
are the **"LOST TRIBES OF ISRAEL."**
Often they came to show him their evidence.
The good Rabbi listened and made no
comment either way.
He figured, as it was, he had several
hundred Jews who did not come to services.
Had he confirmed their evidence, then
he would have several **MILLION "IRISH JEWS"**
who also would not come to services.
So he kept silent.
Yet he told me that with all the logical
evidence they presented, there was even
more than they knew.
FERINSTANCE, there are Irish places that
have pure **HEBREW NAMES.**
These names will not be mentioned here.
For while Ireland has practically no
history of Jewish prejudice,
there might be some reactionaries
who would change these names
to something Gallic like **"SHAMUS."**
SHAMUS in Hebrew means *sexton.*
So you say, "But **SHAMUS** means **JAMES.**"
True, but James means **JACOB,**
which is **ANOTHER** Hebrew name.

The very popular Irish song,
**"DID YOUR MOTHER COME FROM IRELAND,
BECAUSE THERE'S SOMETHING IN YOU IRISH,"**
was written by Michael Carr.
His **REAL** name was Michael Cohen,
an Irish Jew.
One wonders, had Michael been born
in **ENGLAND,** he may have written
a song called,
**"DID YOUR MOTHER COME FROM BRITISH,
BECAUSE THERE'S SOMETHING IN YOU YIDDISH."**

*   *   *   *

The Yiddish word **MENSCH**
means a person.
Not just a person
but a **PERSON PERSON.**
It denotes a **MATURE, INTELLIGENT,
WISE, RESPONSIBLE, SENSIBLE,
RELIABLE, TRUSTWORTHY, LOYAL, KIND,
OBEDIENT, BRAVE, CLEAN,** and **REVERENT**
person.

There is practically no **ONE** English word
that encompasses the entire
idea of what **MENSCH** means.
If anyone finds that word
then **THAT PERSON** is a
MENSCH.
Very few Roger Kaputniks find that word.

The Germans have other ways of using
the word **MENSCH,** such as
UNTERMENSCH—meaning a "nonperson"
and **UBERMENSCH** meaning the **SUPER PERSON.**
JEWS, they said, were **NONPERSONS,**
and they, the Germans, were the **SUPER PERSONS.**
So the Germans threw out such **NONPERSONS AS**
ALBERT EINSTEIN and **MADAME MEITNER,**
who joined up with a bunch of other
JEWISH NONPERSONS
such as the **NONPERSON ROBERT OPPENHEIMER**
        and the
NON PERSON ENRICO FERMI
and all these **NONPERSONS**
produced a **NON-ATOMIC BOMB.**

Meanwhile back at the **RAUNCH,**
THE RAUNCHY SUPER PERSONS
reversed evolution and retreated
back to when primitive persons had
no spoken language,
they spoke with **CLUBS.**

We Americans cannot be smug.
In the year 1857,
our **SUPREME COURT** declared in the
DRED SCOTT DECISION
that all **NEGROES** were **"NONPERSONS."**
In that entire court of **SUPREME PERSONS,**
there wasn't one
"MENSCH" on the bench.

        *   *   *   *

The word **"KIKE"** is used negatively
to describe a Jew.
Where did the word come from?

GOD only knows and **HE** hasn't talked to anyone
        SANE in years.

There are as many theories as to its origin
as there are negative people who
use it negatively.
The theory most theorized is that
when the land of the enslaved
and the home of the coward was programmed
for pogroms—
The Jews left for the land of the free
and the home of the brave.
When they arrived at Ellis Island,
a place where people who were
lost were found,
the Jews were asked to sign
the bureaucratic documents with a cross.
Now, to the Jews, the cross
meant mass crucifixion.
The Romans lined the roads with crucified
Jews like they were sign posts
pointing in four different directions.
Not all roads lead to Rome.
When the Christians adopted
the cross as their religious symbol
it bewildered the Jews.
It was as odd as adopting the gallows
as a religious symbol.
The Jews knew that the true Christian
symbol was a **FISH,** since the first
apostles were Jewish fishermen.

The cross meant to the Jew that it was the
insignia the Crusaders wore, crying,
"KILL A JEW AND SAVE YOUR SOUL."
Many a soul was **"SAVED."**
The Crusaders burned Jews alive in a
Jerusalem synagogue in which Jesus
may have worshipped,
and the synagogue didn't even have fire insurance.
So when the Ellis Island officials
asked the immigrant Jews to sign the
documents with a cross, they refused,
saying they'd sign it with a
"KIKEL,"
which is the Yiddish word for **CIRCLE.**
So whenever a new batch of
Jews arrived, the official named R. Macputnik said,
"Here comes another bunch of them
KIKELS."
A kikel or a circle is a near
perfect thing.
So when a pejorative person calls
a Jew by the negative name of
KIKE, he is really saying he is
NEAR PERFECT.

*   *   *   *

The anthropological terminology for
Caucasian
refers to those white people
who live west of the **CAUCASUS MOUNTAINS**.
There are some of these Caucasians
who say Jews who are white are **NOT CAUCASIANS**
because they came from south of
that **MASONARY DIXON LINE**.
The ones who say this the most
are descendants of the Barbarians
who came from east of that
mountainous racial border line.
When the mountain did not come to the
Barbarians,
The Barbarians came to the mountain —
and went over it.
The Jews went under it.
To **MY FRIEND GOD** a mighty mountain range
is a fingerprint furrow.
MY FRIEND GOD is perfect in
all things, except when it
comes to people,
then **HE**'s **COLORED BLIND**.

*   *   *   *

The old Jewish joke tells about an elderly man
who suddenly keeled over. A crowd quickly formed
around him.
One young fellow named Rogers, who had a
reputation
of being medically knowledgeable, because his
uncle was
a doctor, examined the strickened man.
A Yiddisha momma in the crowd loudly insisted,
"GIVE HIM SOME CHICKEN SOUP!"
The medical mavin answered her with,
"HE'S DEAD! WHAT GOOD WILL THAT DO?"
The Yiddisha momma persisted with,
"IT CAN'T HURT!"

CHICKEN SOUP is internationally known as
"JEWISH PENICILLIN."
It cures **ALL.**
There is some truth that Jewish chicken soup is
a **MIRACLE DRUG.**
This in spite of the scientific fact that chicken
soup contains harmful ingredients such as the
chemical formula
F.A.T.,
which stands for cholesterol.

But it does contain another chemical formula that
is miraculous.
T.L.C.,
which stands for the
TENDER LOVING CARE
in which it is administered.

*　　*　　*　　*

See the people on the beach.
HAPPY people on the beach.
See the things around their necks.
LUCKY THINGS around their necks.
ASTROLOGICAL things around their necks.
ITALIAN HORNS around their necks.
TIKI IDOLS around their necks.
ANKHS around their necks.
CHAIS around their necks.
CHAI is the **EIGHTEENTH** letter
around the **HEBREW** alphabet.
CHAI means **LIFE** around the Hebrew community.
See how all those other things
around their necks ward off evil spirits,
evil eyes, guarantee enduring life
and lucky months around their necks.
See the people on the beach.
Are they **HAPPY** people on the beach?
Are they **RELIGIOUS** people on the beach?
Peel off a layer of sunburnt skin.
Hear the people yell, **"OUCH!"**
See beneath the outer layer.
See **PRIMITIVE, SUPERSTITIOUS, NEUROTIC**
people on the beach
See the age they live in.
Hear how it's called **"ANXIETY."**
See the **UNHAPPY** people on the beach.
See the things they wear around their necks.
Are they **RELIGIOUS SYMBOLS** around their necks?
No, they are **GODLESS PAGAN** things
around their necks.
See Roger get uptight.

Hear Roger yell,
**"JUST ONE BIG FAT MINUTE!
GOD IS OMNIPOTENT. RIGHT?
GOD IS EVERYWHERE. RIGHT?
SO GOD IS IN THOSE PAGAN IDOLS.
RIGHT?"**
Hear Roger almost be **RIGHT**.
See the **HAPPY** people on the beach.
See the **HOLY SYMBOLS** around their necks.
See the **LUCKY CHARMS** around their necks.

But what good is it to just have
A LUCKY NECK?

*　　*　　*　　*

I am not an Orthodox Jew,
nor a Conservative Jew,
nor a Reform Jew,
nor a Reconstructionist Jew,
I am a *Jew*.
So when I see my co-religionists quarrel
and live in separate rooms,
I am **TROUBLED**.
A house divided—
is probably a **SPLIT LEVEL**,
with a **KOSHER KITCHEN**,
and a *trefe* **DEEP FREEZE**.
When a non-Jewish people-hater sneers
at a member of a Reform Temple
and says,
"YOU'RE A JEW!"
then a member of an Orthodox Schule
says to the same man,
"YOU'RE *NOT* A JEW!"

this gives him an *identity crisis.*
Is it any wonder then that,
with us Jews, being **NEUROTIC
IS NORMAL?**

During the **UNCHRISTIAN** era,
when Catholics and Protestants
were at each others' throats,
trying to *tear off each others' crucifixes,*
each trying to prove who was the **ONLY AND TRUE
          WAY,**
each trying to prove who was more **RIGHTEOUS,**
by who
SHALT KILL
more than the other,
then the Jewish observers said,
"IT'S A SHANDEH!" (a shame).
Are we Jews also becoming **UNCHRISTIAN?**
And are the Christian observers saying,
"IT'S A SHANDEH!"?

*   *   *   *

Before Pope John XXIII,
before Catholics became Christian,
my Jewish kinsman roomed at college
with a lad of the papacy persuasion.
My kinsman invited his roomie to attend
a synagogue.
The roomie informed him that his church
did not allow him to go to the Houses of
GOD of either the Jews or the Protestants.

My kinsman who knows of no other prejudice
except when an orthodox Jew occasionally
referred to a reform Jew with a **"YEECCCH,"**
disbelieved him.
To prove the point, the Catholic boy instructed
my kin on the proper ritual.
Then he took him to a Catholic Church
and into a confessional booth.
"Father, forgive me, for I have sinned,"
said my Jewish relation.
"I have attended services in a synagogue."
This was no lie.
The priest was horrified and berated him.
"For your sin you must do *penance.*
Say *seven Hail Marys.*"
So my Jewish relative apologized seven times
for attending a Jewish synagogue
to the Jewish Mary
**WHO HAD ATTENDED A JEWISH SYNAGOGUE
        HERSELF.**

*   *   *   *

*   *   *   *

The old story tells about Ivan the Terrible.
On a holy day
he went to a holy man
and said,
**"PROVE TO ME THERE IS A GOD, IN
TWO WORDS."**
And the holy man
on a holy day said,
"THE JEWS."

The new story tells about Roger the terrible.
On a holy day
he went to a holy man
and said,
"Why don't the Jews build
THE THIRD TEMPLE?"
"They have," said the holy man.
**"TELL ME WHAT IS IT, IN
ONE WORD."**
And the holy man
on a holy day said,
"ISRAEL."

*   *   *   *

A college newspaper reporter once threw a hand
        grenade
at me in the form of a question.

"Would you mind if your daughter married
a **BLACK** man?"
The explosion scrambled my brains, and my
befuddled answer was,
"Not at all, as long as he's **JEWISH**."

After the dispersion, the Jews wandered
GOD only knows where.
Some archaeologists say they know what
GOD knows, claiming there is evidence
that the Jews were in South America
and in the Midwest of the now United States
long before another former Jew named
Columbus sailed off the edge of the world
and found America.
GOD MUST be everywhere,
because **JEWS** are everywhere.
When Mars becomes a local stop on
the weekend excursion, one may
calculate this future problem.
A future yenta might say to a future
        Mrs. Solomon Kaputnik,
"I hear your daughter married a Martian.
        That's terrible."
"It's not so terrible," the future
        Mrs. Solomon Kaputnik might say.
"He's **JEWISH**."
That's not just being a wandering Jew,
THAT'S BEING FABLUNGGED.

*   *   *   *

*   *   *   *

Often it has been asked of me
why so many other peoples
produce so many alcoholics
yet the Jews produce practically **NONE**.
After **SOBERING UP**,
I finally figured it out.
An ancient proverb says:
"**GOD BESTOWED TWO GIFTS UPON MAN.
TO SOME HE GAVE THE GIFT OF WINE,
AND TO SOME THE FACULTY OF THIRST.**"
The Jews have the gift of wine,
they **MANISCHEWITZED AND
MOGEN DAVIDED IT.**
But rarely do they have the gift of thirst.
Why?
Wine plays such a large part
in Jewish religious ritual.
Before one drinks the wine,
he must go through the ritual
of saying a prayer in **HEBREW**,
which translates to,
"**BLESSED ART THOU, LORD OF
THE UNIVERSE, FOR GIVING US
THE FRUIT OF THE VINE.**"
By the time a Jew gets
to the third glass and he has to
go through the whole prayer, in disgust he says,
"**OH, TO HELL WITH IT!**"
and doesn't take the drink.
That way they never get to
become alcoholics.

My suggestion for the alcoholic-
producing ethnic group is,
introduce the Jewish practice of
MANDATORILY and **RELIGIOUSLY** saying that
        prayer before
drinking a glass of alcoholic beverage,
and in Hebrew,
**"BORUCH ATOH ADONOY, ELOHAYNOO MELECH
        HOOLOM,
BORAY, P'REE HAGOFEN."**
By the time Roger McKaputnik
gets to the third glass,
he'll stumble and fumble over the
unfamiliar Hebrew words.
Finally, in disgust, he'll claim
the whole thing is a damn
JEWISH PLOT. He'll spend an
hour **TIRADING AGAINST THE
JEWS.** And never get around
to taking that third drink,
SAVING HIM FROM ALCOHOLISM.

*   *   *   *

There are some Catholics who have a
great **CONFESSION** to make—
Not in the privacy of the womblike
confessional booth—
but to the **WORLD.**
They wish to confess that
**"CATHOLIC CONFESSION IS NOT CATHOLIC
IT'S JEWISH."**
On **YOM KIPPUR,** the Day of Atonement for Jews,
the entire synagogue becomes a large
CONFESSIONAL BOOTH.
The congregation rises and recites
the prayer called **"A GUIDE TO THE
OPENING OF THE HEART,"**
a portion of which reads thusly:
"The sin we have sinned against **THEE,** under
stress or through choice. . . the sin
which we have sinned against **THEE**
openly or in secret . . . in stubbornness
or in error in the evil meditations
of the heart . . . by word of mouth . . .
profanation of power . . . disrespect
for parents and teachers . . . by exploiting
and dealing treacherously with our
neighbor. . . . For all these Sins,
O GOD of Forgiveness, bear with us, pardon us,
forgive us."
Then, silent confessions are made, with
a beating of the breast.
When a Catholic Priest beats his breast,
he is continuing the tradition of
the Jews who have been
BREASTING IN PEACE
with the same gesture for thousands of years.

There is one other mammal that confesses
in this manner—
THE GORILLA.
When some other small animal,
like an elephant,
invades his lair, the gorilla
BEATS HIS BREAST.
Zoologists tell us this is to frighten
off the intruder.
Not so.
When the gorilla beats his breast
on such occasions, he is confessing
to **GOD** that he's not a gorilla,
HE'S CHICKEN.

Yom Kippur is not the only day of confession
for the Jews. There are periods of
meditation in most services wherein
one can confess
or think thoughts.
This can lead to other periods of meditation
when confession will be made about
the thoughts thunk.
Catholics confess to **GOD**
through a man with a Theological Degree—
FREE OF CHARGE.

Some Jews confess **DIRECTLY** to **GOD**—
FREE OF CHARGE.
Other Jews go to a man with a psychiatric
degree and cathartically confess their sin
FOR A CHARGE.
So while **THEIR** confession is **GOOD FOR THE SOUL,**
it's **BETTER FOR THE SHRINK.**

*   *   *   *

CRITICIZE! CRITICIZE! That's all you ever do is CRITICIZE! Can't you ever say anything NICE about me?
Well . . . ?
I'm thinking . . .
About the only nice thing I can say about you is that your "In-Laws" are nicer than my "In-Laws"!
Okay! At least you admit it!
HEY, WAIT A MINUTE!! . . . WHAT DID YOU SAY . . . ??
Berg

The old story tells about this married couple
who moved into a new apartment that was
built right over the subway.
That night when they went to sleep,
every time the subway cars passed
beneath them, the rumbling bounced them
out of bed.
The first thing, the next morning,
the wife sent for the janitor.
She loudly complained about the **DEBEDDING.**
The janitor said,
"I don't believe you."
"Okay, I'll prove it," said the agitated woman.
"You get on one side of the bed
and I'll get on the other side. Just
you watch what happens when a
subway train passes beneath us."
So the janitor and the woman
prostrated themselves on the bed.
Just then the husband walked in
and shouted,
"WHAT ARE YOU DOING IN BED WITH MY WIFE?"
The innocent janitor stammered,
"WOULD YOU BELIEVE I'M WAITING FOR A TRAIN?"

Would you believe that there are many innocent
people waiting for the right Messiah in the
wrong place?
And so this tale is told
that a rumor swept the world
that on such and such a day
on such and such an hour,
such and such a **MESSIAH**
would come.

"BUT WHERE WOULD HE ARRIVE?"

was the question.
And everybody said,
"In such and such a place."
The Catholics said,
"He was a Jew, he would go to the synagogue."
So all the Catholics rushed to such and
such synagogue.
And the Protestants said,
"But he was the founder of the
Catholic Church, he would go to Mass."
So all the Protestants rushed to
such and such a cathedral.
And the Jews said,
"Maybe such and such is the Messiah.
He was a protestor, so he would
go to a Protestant Church."
So all the Jews rushed to such and such
Protestant Church.
That such and such day came
and the such and such hour struck
and that such and such Messiah
CAME TO NONE of those such and such
places.
And all the people were like the innocent
janitor, lying in the wrong bed,
waiting for the right train in the
wrong place.
And all those doubting, faithless
followers climbed back into their
own beds.
Had such and such a Messiah
come as rumored,
and had he come as some have predicted,
on a **FIERY CHARIOT,**
than he would find no place

to **PARK.**
And some policeman named Roger Coputnik
would give him a ticket for driving
an **UNSAFE VEHICLE.**

*　　　*　　　*　　　*

One of the most basic principles of Christianity is,
**"IF HE SMITE THEE ON ONE CHEEK,
TURN THE OTHER."**
It was authored by a Jew named Jesus
who spoke in tongues.
The tongue being Aramaic, a modern form of Hebrew.
In theory it is a perfect practice.
But practice makes perfect.
It wasn't practice enough
or at all.
When one Christian country invades another
　　　　　Christian
country, smiting, burning, looting, and raping a city—
the invadee **DID NOT TURN THE OTHER CHEEK**
　　　　　and say,
"S'all right, we have another city to turn to you
that needs **ZERO POPULATION GROWTH."**
Instead they zeroed in on the invaders' city
and spread birth control by using the
SWORD as a **CONTRACEPTIVE.**

When a knight wearing a Crusader's cross
threw down the gauntlet to another
crusading knight as a challenge to mortal combat,
the challenged knight **DID NOT TURN THE
OTHER CHEEK** and say,

"S'all right, throw down the other gauntlet."
No, he threw down the challenging knight
with lance, battle axe, sword, spiked chain,
and other instruments of peace.
When a Protestant Church attacked
a Catholic Church,
the Catholics didn't turn the other cheek
and say
"S'all right, as long as you didn't do it on
BINGO NIGHT."
No, the Catholic Church **BINGOED** the Protestant
        Church.

But when a practicing Christian wished to practice
turning the other cheek
HE SMITE A JEW.
THE JEW DID THE CHEEK-TURNING.

The last time the Jews **DID NOT**
do any cheek-turning was at
MASADA in 90 A.D. For the next 1,858 years,
the Jews turned their cheeks like
their necks were **GREASED WITH CHICKEN FAT,**
        saying,
"S'all right, they'll get tired soon and stop.
We'll outlive the cheek smiters.
Get out the chicken fat,
grease the neck
and **START TURNING.**"
And they say Jews are a **STIFF-NECKED PEOPLE!**
But in the Warsaw Ghetto of 1943,
The Jews realized
IT WAS NOT ALL RIGHT.

The Nazis were not going to get tired.
They were not going to stop
The Jews were not going to outlive
the cheek smiters.
And they were not going to turn
the other cheek.
Instead they turned Passover wine
bottles into Molotov cocktails and gave
the Nazis a Matzah Fry.
And the Nazis said,
"HOW THOROUGHLY UNCHRISTIAN OF THE JEWS."
So in order to be a practicing Christian
by **TURNING** the other cheek,
you must first be **JEWISH,**
the way we *were* once.

If I have offended a practicing Christian
by a painful truth, and they wish to do the
UNCHRISTIAN thing by smiting me on the cheek,
I will turn the other, on which is written,
"NEVER AGAIN!"

*   *   *   *

MAD—Jan., 1962

I guess they're
not very religious!

Berg

When I was this skinny little Jewish kid,
I was passing this parochial elementary school
just as those Irish Catholic
kids came running out
yelling at me,
"PERFIDIOUS JEW."
My adrenalin gushed with rage.
Why?
Because they knew what
PERFIDIOUS meant.
And I didn't.

Many years later,
my favorite Pope,
John the XXIII, said to those Irish kids,
**"DAT'S NOTTA NICE
TO SAY SUCH WORDS!"**

But I was still pretty uptight
about the matter.

In the early 1970's I decided
to take some refresher courses.
And what was the nearest college
to me?
**IONA, A CATHOLIC PAROCHIAL SCHOOL
RUN BY IRISH CHRISTIAN BROTHERS.
OY, VAY!**
My first day of theology class,
being a real Roger Kaputnik,
I wasn't just uptight. My hairs hurt as if they were all
exposed nerve endings.
In walks this big Irish Christian
Brother Michael,
he opens his mouth to speak
and out comes,

**"EVERYTHING YOU LEARNED IN PAROCHIAL
         SCHOOL IS
WRONG. WE ARE A NEW CHURCH. CATHOLICISM
IS BASED ON THE JEWISH TORAH. THERE'S NO
SUCH THING AS THE OLD TESTAMENT. IT'S
         THE BIBLE.
MOST OF OUR MASS IS BASED ON LEVITICUS
AND THE PASSOVER SEDER. WE OWE EVERYTHING
TO THE JEWS."**

Being the only Jew in the room,
the entire class turned toward me,
fell on their knees
and **GENUFLECTED.**

Brother Michael had a very
simple marking system.
All the Irish students got **A**'s.
All the Italian students got **B**'s.
And all the other ethnic students
FAILED.
Except me, the only Jew in the class,
I was **SAINTED.**

Shortly after the semester ended,
the soul of Brother Michael
suddenly left this polluted earth
FOR A BETTER PLACE.

In grief, I could think of
nothing else to do
but don my yamulke
and prayer shawl.
In faltering Hebrew I recited
the prayer for the dead
called **KADDISH.**

My friend, the Irish **CHRISTIAN
BROTHER MICHAEL BRADLEY** (alovishsholom)
would have liked that.

Before he died, I showed this script to Brother
Michael. He approved.
I regret that I had to add the last passage.

REST IN PEACE, BROTHER MICHAEL.

*　　*　　*　　*

IS GOD AN ATHEIST?

A twice-told tale tells about
a group of scientists who developed
the **ULTIMATE COMPUTER.**
They decided therefore to ask
the **ULTIMATE QUESTION:**
"IS THERE A GOD?"

The computer whirred, clicked,
and all its lights blinked.
Finally the message appeared;
it said,
"NOW THERE IS!"

To some scientists a computer
is **GOD.**
But a computer knows only
what a scientist programmed it for
and the scientist knows
only what **GOD** programmed him for.

So if in the past you had doubts as to whether
there was a **GOD,**
let me assure you.
NOW THERE IS.
AND HE WAS BEFORE.
AND BEFORE GOD WAS. . . .
GOD WAS.

*   *   *   *

When there is no other way,
There is still a way—
GOD!
If you don't take that way,
GOD HELP YOU!
So there is **STILL** a way.

*   *   *   *

GOD has many names,
among which **NONE** of them
is **HOWARD**.
In spite of what the kids say
when they recite:
"Our Father Which Art in Heaven
HOWARD Be Thy Name."

The opening line of this "Christian"
prayer the kids are trying to say
comes from an ancient **HEBREW**
prayer the Orthodox Jews recite
twice daily.
Which only goes to prove:

"Roses are red,
violets and bluish,
I love you,
and the **WHOLE WORLD IS JEWISH**."

When we Roger Kaputniks are in trouble
and need to call on **GOD'S** help,
we don't know how to look **HIM** up
in the telephone book,
because **GOD** has an
UNLISTED TELEPHONE NUMBER.

*   *   *   *

There are those who say,
"GOD IS LOVE."
There are those who say,
"GOD IS RITUAL."
Some of us Roger Kaputniks say,
"GOD IS MITZVAH."
THE GOOD DEED is done in **SECRET,**
or else it becomes **NULL** and **VOID.**
But a **MITZVAH** must also be **PASSED ON,**
and in **SECRET,**
so **GOD** is
THE BEST-KEPT SECRET IN THE WORLD.
Which is what is meant by,
"Don't let your right hand know
what your left hand is doing."
An easy feat to accomplish,
EXCEPT WHEN YOU'RE WASHING YOUR HANDS!

What is an example of a Kaputnik-type Mitzvah?
When a husband and wife are having a fight,
And Roger **BUTTS OUT,** and doesn't tell
anyone he **BUTT OUT,**
THAT'S A MITZVAH.
EARN A MITZVAH TODAY,
          MINDYOUROWNDAMNBUZINEZZ.
A Regina Kaputnik-type **MITZVAH**
is a person who visits sick friends,
and doesn't tell anyone about it.
Reginas make very good **NURSES,**
but very **BAD FRIENDS.**
THEY NEVER COME WHEN YOU ARE WELL.
Visiting a **WELL** person is also a **MITZVAH,**
because everyone in the world is,
SICK! SICK! SICK!
So earn a **MITZVAH** today,
  DON'T MINDYOUROWNDAMNBUZINEZZ.

After the Nazis resigned from
the **HUMAN RACE**,
after they decimated **GOD'S CHOSEN PEOPLE**,
after they killed more Jews in Europe
than existed at the time in the whole
United States,
after the Nazis declared being **"CHOSEN"**
a crime punishable by mass death,
after they interpreted the biblical quotation
of chosen being a **"BLESSING AND A CURSE,"**
after they forgot the **BLESSING** and
remembered the **CURSE**,
then many disillusioned Jews said,
"The **NEW TESTAMENT SAYS TO
'FORGIVE SEVENTY TIMES SEVEN.'**
But can we forgive
SIX MILLION?

Therefore, **GOD** was, **BUT IS NO MORE.
HE WAS CREMATED IN AUSCHWITZ."**

It took Nietzche and a group of Protestants
to give this negative thinking a name.

"GOD IS DEAD."

They said **HE** no longer is in Heaven,
and **HE** no longer reigns supreme.
It used to be that **PLACES**
were **GOD FORSAKEN.**
Today, it's **GOD'S PLACE**
that is **FORSAKEN.**

WELL, GOD IS DEAD!
GOD'S nourishment is **MITZVAH.**
HE died of **STARVATION.**

There were too many children
who ate their favorite food,
THEIR PARENTS' HEARTS.
While nourishing themselves,
they earned no **MITZVAHS,**
and denied **GOD** his nourishment.

And **GOD LOST WEIGHT!**

There were too few people
who did a favor for someone

KNOWING
that they'd never get a
THANK YOU,
but a kick in the groin instead,
yet still went ahead and
DID IT!
Most people would call this schlemiel-
type person a
SCHLEMIEL.
GOD loved this **SCHLEMIEL-**
type **MITZVAH.**

But this tasty tidbit
was so very very **RARE,**
and **ALWAYS OUT OF SEASON.**
And **GOD** said,

"I HUNGER."

Too many people committed
ANTI-MITZVAHS
with their people's
inhumanity to people.
In extreme cruelty
they wished on other
human beings the
SUPREME CURSE.
"MAY YOU BE THE
PARENTS OF TEEN-AGERS
GOING THROUGH AN
IDENTITY CRISIS."

And **GOD** famished.

There were too few men who did not
listen to H.L. Mencken's advice:
"At least once in your life,
wink at a homely girl."
That's a Mitzvah morsel
GOD was denied,

and **GOD** weakened.

They said **TECHNOLOGY** has **REPLACED GOD**.
And churches and synagogues are
emptier than ever.
Kaputnik families are staying home
instead and watching the **TECHNOLOGY OF
TELEVISION** where they listen to clergymen
repeat the **WORDS OF GOD**
before **HE** was **REPLACED**.

Mitzvah used to be a personal
virtue.
Today it's an **ORGANIZATION,**
such as Zionism,
which the old joke describes as:
"One Jew asking another Jew
for money to send a third
Jew to Israel."
That's half a Mitzvah.
Half a loaf is better than none,

and **GOD** momentarily rallied.

Then there are the
ANTI-ZIONISTS.

**KID YOURSELF NOT.
ANTI-ZIONISM IS A
EUPHEMISM FOR THE
FINAL SOLUTION,**

which is a non-mitzvah,

and **GOD** suffered a relapse.

**IF THE WORLD WON'T LET ISRAEL LIVE,
THAN NO ONE WILL LIVE.
IF GOD CAN DIE, SO CAN THE WORLD.**

In the **UNITED STATES OF AMERICA . . .**
Too many phones were bugged
TO ASSURE FREEDOM OF SPEECH.
Too many kids went to **POT**
and took **DRUGS** like they were vitamins.
Too many **ADULTS** were driven to **PILLS** and **DRINK,**
which was no **DRIVE**
but a **SHORT WALK.**
Too many **CRIMES** were committed
like they were **MITZVAHS.**
Too many **STATISTICS** showed
DIVORCES outnumbered **MARRIAGES.**
Too many **SATANIC CULTS** existed
that even the **DEVIL** was afraid to join.
Too many **FALSE CLAIMS** were filed
for **WELFARE** for the **INDOLENT.**
And too many **FALSE CLAIMS** of
TAX SHELTERS
which was **WELFARE FOR THE AFFLUENT.**
Too many of the **GAY**
said that the world began with
ADAM and **ADAM.**

Too many of the **STRAIGHT**
discussed the **IMMORALITY** of **HOMOSEXUALITY**
          at **ORGIES.**
Too many took part in **HUSBAND SWAPPINGS**
only to discover that **VARIETY WAS NOT**
THE SPICE OF WIFE.
Too many **COUPLES**
lived together without getting **HITCHED**
and found that **THAT WAS THE HITCH.**
There were **TOO MANY,**
TOO MUCH,
in the **LAND OF PLENTY**—
an overabundance of
NON-MITZVAHS.
And the name of the land was changed to
THE UNITED SODOM OF GOMORRAH.

And **GOD RETCHED** and took to **HIS SICK BED,**
which was as large as **HALF A UNIVERSE.**
And **HE** wasn't even covered by
BLUE CROSS.

Too many of the young and healthy
took vows of **POVERTY AND NO WORK.**
A luxury only the children
of the **NOUVEAU-MIDDLE CLASS**
could afford.
Idleness corrupts, and
total idleness
corrupts totally.
Too many of those **NOUVEAU**-Roger Kaputnik-
type permissive parents
held their tempers
by counting to **TEN**—
one for each commandment
they broke.
Too many **NEW** powers were given to these
NOUVEAUS!
POWER CORRUPTS
AND TOTAL MIDDLE CLASS POWER
CORRUPTS MILDLY.

There were too many old and unhealthy
who took **NO** vows of poverty
and could not work.
A luxury only the very poor could afford.
**POVERTY CORRUPTS
AND TOTAL POVERTY
CORRUPTS TOTALLY.**
If those young and healthy who took vows
of poverty
had taken vows of **MITZVAHS** instead,
then the **POOR WOULD NOT
ALWAYS BE WITH US.**
Only the **STUPID** are **ETERNAL**.

**AND GOD LINGERED, AND GOD CRIED,
"GOD HELP ME."**
and **GOD** could not.

**MITZVAH INTERRUPTS
AND TOTAL MITZVAH INTERRUPTS
STARVATION TOTALLY.**

There were too many kids
who said,
"LIKE, MAN, I NEED A FIX BAD."
And some stupid kid
gave him the fix.
When the first kid
O.D.'d,
the second kid said,
"I was only trying to earn
a **MITZVAH."**

And **GOD** became more
EMACIATED.

There were too many kids
who said,
"I'M FOR PEACE, THAT'S A MITZVAH,
then became **HAWKS** for the
OTHER SIDE.

And **GOD** went into
INTENSIVE CARE,
where **HE** wasn't even fed **MITZVAHS** intravenously.

GOD'S last words were,
"When **I** created the world,
I said,
it was **'GOOD.'**
It is no longer."

And so, **GOD DIED!**
GOD IS DEAD!

HE died of **MALNUTRITION.**
He fed on
not enough vitamins
A, B, C, D, and **E.**
But an overdose

of **I** and **ME.**
Such as,
**"I COME FIRST AND TO
HELL WITH EVERYONE ELSE"**
and
**"WHAT'S IN IT FOR
ME?"**
GOD is **MITZVAH.**
Without **MITZVAH,**
GOD IS NO MORE.

SO HE DIED!

**AND WENT ALL THE WAY UP TO HEAVEN,
EVEN HIGHER THAN HEAVEN,
WHERE HE REIGNS SUPREME.**

**THAT'S GOD'S MITZVAH.
WHICH IS OUR
NOURISHMENT.**

THANK GOD THAT GOD LIVES.

**AND THANK GOD THAT THERE ARE
SO MANY ROGER KAPUTNIKS
WHO FEED GOD
SECRETLY!**

*   *   *   *

*   *   *   *

So now we know who **GOD** is.
GOD IS MITZVAH.

But who is
ROGER KAPUTNIK?
It's the **SCHLEMIEL**
in all of us,
with a legacy—
TO INHERIT THIS POLLUTED EARTH.

*   *   *   *

More Humor from SIGNET

☐ **HIP KIDS' LETTERS FROM CAMP by Bill Adler; illustrated by Howie Schneider.** It's a groove, it's a wild trip, it's Bill Adler's newest and nuttiest mailbag collection from those far-out campers! (#T5483—75¢)

☐ **YOU'RE IN LOVE, CHARLIE BROWN by Charles M. Schulz.** Charlie Brown in love? Why not? Watch out for that pretty little red-haired girl! (#T4282—75¢)

☐ **MORE LETTERS FROM CAMP edited by Bill Adler.** One of America's foremost collectors of modern humor, Bill Adler, joins forces with cartoonist Sid Hoff in a book playfully devoted to the foibles of the young fry.
(#T5650—75¢)

☐ **WEE PALS, GETTING IT ALL TOGETHER.** The fourth in this series of delightful cartoons, a book for children of all ages! (#T5376—75¢)

☐ **CHARLIE BROWN'S ALL STARS by Charles M. Schulz.** Linus, Lucy, Frieda, Shermy, Snoopy and Charlie Brown himself—the whole team that delights millions of fans in the popular cartoon strip are on deck in this story of an all-star baseball team and its conscientious but misunderstood manager. In full color. (#T4256—75¢)

Other SIGNET Books You'll Enjoy

☐ **WEE PALS: STAYING COOL by Morrie Turner.** The "KID POWER" gang is back! Those colorful cartoon kids will get you grinning again at their latest hilarious adventures.   (#T6076—75¢)

☐ **STILL MORE LETTERS FROM CAMP.** Bestselling collector of humor, Bill Adler, and cartoonist, Syd Hoff, once again join forces to bring you this hilarious new gathering of gems from the kids at camp.   (#T5651—75¢)

☐ **WEE PALS: KID POWER by Morrie Turner.** Children from multi-racial backgrounds meet life head-on while their "wiser" elders grope self-consciously through the muddles they create for themselves.   (#T5344—75¢)

☐ **PLAY IT AGAIN, CHARLIE BROWN by Charles M. Schulz.** Rumor has it that Schroeder is abandoning Beethoven for rock. The Beethoven fan club is shuddering. Lucy is smiling in triumph. Charlie Brown, Linus, and Snoopy are forming a band to back Schroeder up. And the whole country is rocking with fun and laughter at this latest, greatest caper of Charlie Brown and the whole Peanuts gang! In full color.   (#T5200—75¢)

☐ **HE'S YOUR DOG, CHARLIE BROWN by Charles M. Schulz.** Poor Snoopy is being sent back to obedience school and the result is a warm, wonderful story.
                                                       (#T4691—75¢)

Still More Humor from SIGNET

☐ **LOVE IS by Kim Grove.**   (#T6198—75¢)

☐ **MORE LOVE IS by Kim Grove.**   (#T6199—75¢)

☐ **LOVE IS #3 by Kim Grove.**   (#T6200—75¢)

☐ **LOVE IS #4 by Kim Grove.**   (#T6201—75¢)

☐ **LOVE IS #5 by Kim Grove.**   (#T6202—75¢)

☐ **LOVE IS #6 by Kim Grove.**   (#T6203—75¢)

☐ **LOVE IS #7 by Kim Grove.**   (#T6126—75¢)

☐ **LOVE IS #8 by Kim Grove.**   (#T5938—75¢)

☐ **LOVE IS #9 by Kim Grove.**   (#T6077—75¢)

☐ **LOVE IS #10 by Kim Grove.**   (#T6107—75¢)